Walk Worthy

Walk Worthy

by
John MacArthur, Jr.

WORD OF GRACE COMMUNICATIONS
P.O. Box 4000
Panorama City, CA 91412

Contents

These Bible studies are taken from messages delivered by Pastor-Teacher John MacArthur, Jr., at Grace Community Church in Panorama City, California. These messages have been combined into a 6-tape album titled *Walk Worthy*. You may purchase this series either in an attractive vinyl cassette album or as individual cassettes. To purchase these tapes, request the album *Walk Worthy*, or ask for the tapes by their individual GC numbers. Please consult the current price list; then, send your order, making your check payable to:

WORD OF GRACE COMMUNICATIONS
P.O. Box 4000
Panorama City, CA 91412

Or call the following toll-free number:
1-800-55-GRACE

1
The Lowly Walk—Part 1

Outline

Lesson
I. The Principle of Conformity
   A. Conformity to Social Standards
      1. The pledge
      2. The penalty
      3. The pitfall
   B. Conformity to Biblical Standards
      1. The problem
      2. The penalty
II. The Purpose of God's Calling
   A. Our Practice in Christ
      1. 1 Peter 2:15
      2. Philippians 1:27
   B. Our Position in Christ
III. The Pattern of Paul's Transition
   A. In Romans
      1. Duty
      2. Doctrine
   B. In Galatians
   C. In Philippians
   D. In Colossians
IV. The Priority of Knowledge
   A. The Search for Wisdom
      1. Job 28:1-12
      2. Proverbs 2:4-6
      3. Colossians 1:9-10

B. The Source of Renewal
   1. Ephesians 1:17
   2. Philippians 1:9-10
   3. Colossians 1:10
   4. Colossians 3:10
   5. 2 Peter 3:18
   6. Colossians 1:28
   7. 2 Timothy 3:16-17
C. The State of the Church

Conclusion

Lesson

I. THE PRINCIPLE OF CONFORMITY

   A. Conformity to Social Standards

      1. The pledge

         People who live in a society are obligated to act in accordance with the standards of that society. For example, a person who chooses to live in the United States is expected to abide by the principles, standards, and laws that govern the United States. Employees are expected to conform to the standards and objectives of their particular employer. If you join a club or athletic team, you are asked to uphold certain principles.

      2. The penalty

         If a person doesn't conform to the standards set by his social structure, he will lose his position within the framework of that organization. He becomes a hindrance to the society and is dismissed from it. If you break the law, you will be incarcerated. If you don't do the job your employer hired you to do, you will be fired. If you are a member of an athletic team and don't follow the coach's instructions, you will be kicked off the team.

3. The pitfall

The principle of conformity can become extremely binding for some people. Most of us want to be team players. That's a healthy part of human nature—wanting to belong and to gain acceptance. But that desire can become obsessive. John 9:1-23 is a good illustration of that. The Lord Jesus Christ performed a wonderful miracle: He healed a man who had been born blind. Jesus spit in some clay, made a little mud, put it on the blind man's eyes, and told him to wash in the pool of Siloam. The man did so and returned having gained his sight (vv. 7-8). The religious leaders began to investigate this miracle. They talked to the blind man's parents, who said, "By what means he now seeth, we know not; or who hath opened his eyes, we know not. He is of age; ask him. He shall speak for himself" (v. 21). Even though they knew better, they wouldn't acknowledge how he was healed. They wouldn't give credit to Jesus Christ or glorify God. They didn't want to get involved "because they feared the [Jewish leaders]; for [they] had agreed already that, if any man did confess that he was the Christ, he should be put out of the synagogue" (v. 22). The blind man's parents were so constrained by their desire for acceptance in their society that they wouldn't give credit to Christ for their son's miraculous healing. The things with which people identify can become so binding that they become blind to reality. In this case the parents were blind to the glory of Christ.

When I was young I wanted to join fraternities and certain clubs. In the process, I had to endure the most incredible initiations you can imagine. I look back on those days and wonder what possessed me to pursue those things. The drive to belong is very strong. People often will do anything to conform to principles of a secret society because they want so desperately to be accepted—they need an identity.

B. Conformity to Biblical Standards

1. The problem

Many people in the church want the blessings, rights, and privileges of being a child of God; yet they're unwilling to conform to biblical standards. To them the need to conform to God's standards doesn't seem as binding as the need to achieve worldly pursuits. Perhaps the reason is that Satan reinforces commitment to unimportant standards in his worldly organizations, while he attempts to subvert commitment to biblical standards in Christians.

2. The penalty

When a person believes in Jesus Christ and receives salvation, Christ bestows on him all the rights, honors, and privileges that come with being a Christian. But He also wants him to conform to His standards. The New Testament is clear on what happens to the professing believer who doesn't conform to those standards. First Corinthians 5:1-8 says that if someone in the church is living in an immoral manner, he is to be put out of the church. Second Thessalonians 3:6 says that if someone in the church is living an unruly life and is not responding to counsel, he is to be put out of the church. And 1 Timothy 6:3-5 says that if someone is teaching doctrine inconsistent with the truth of God, he is to be put out of the church.

Sometimes the Lord puts out such people on His own. Some immoral members of the Corinthian church became weak or sick, and some even died (1 Cor. 11:30). First John 5:16 refers to a "sin unto death," where the Lord permanently excommunicates a believer engaged in habitual, premeditated sin.

If people can rigidly conform to the standards of a relatively important group, certainly Christians ought to be able to make a commitment to walk in the manner God desires.

II. THE PURPOSE OF GOD'S CALLING

A. Our Practice in Christ

In the last three chapters of the book of Ephesians, the apostle Paul exhorts believers to commit themselves to God's calling. Ephesians 4:1 begins, "I therefore, the prisoner of the Lord, beseech you that ye walk worthy of the vocation to which ye are called." In Ephesians 1-3 Paul discusses the rights, honors, and privileges of the believer. In the last three chapters he gives the requirements—the standards by which we are to live.

When we entered the Body of Christ, our Lord gave us rights, privileges, and honors. He granted us "the riches of his glory" (Eph. 3:16). He "blessed us with all spiritual blessings in heavenly places" (1:3). And in ages to come He will pour out "his grace in his kindness toward us" (2:7). Based on all that Christ has done for us, Paul tells us what He expects of us: to walk worthy of such a calling. The Lord expects us to act like members of His Body—to make His goals and objectives our goals and objectives. He expects us to be like Him.

1. 1 Peter 2:15—The apostle Peter said, "So is the will of God, that with well-doing ye may put to silence the ignorance of foolish men." We ought to silence our critics by our godly lifestyle. Unfortunately many Christians don't walk worthy of their calling.

2. Philippians 1:27—Paul said, "Let your conduct be as it becometh the gospel of Christ."

B. Our Position in Christ

The first three chapters of Ephesians present positional truth. God has given us incredible resources and riches. He chose us in Him before the foundation of the world to be holy and blameless (1:4). He predestinated us in love and adopted us (1:5). He made us to the praise of His glory and accepted us in Christ, the Beloved (1:6). He provided re-

11

demption and forgiveness for us (1:7). He gave us wisdom (1:8). He made known to us the mystery of His will (1:9). In the future He will give us the inheritance He planned before the world began (1:10-11). He gave us the Holy Spirit (1:13) and resurrection power (1:19-20). He made us alive though we were dead (2:1). We who were at one time lost and cut off from God have been made into one new man in Himself (2:13-15). He gave us understanding of a great mystery: that of Jew and Gentile being united by the gospel in the church (3:3-6). He made it possible for us to capitalize on all those things by strengthening us with His Holy Spirit so that Christ can dwell in our hearts (3:17), so that we can be filled with His incomprehensible love (3:18), be filled with the fullness of God (3:19), and can know His power (3:20). Rightly does Paul tell us in the next chapter to walk worthy—to live up to what God has given us. Our identity in Christ dictates our lifestyle.

III. THE PATTERN OF PAUL'S TRANSITION

The transition Paul makes between chapters 3 and 4 is not random. It was typical for Paul to make a transition from doctrine to duty, from principle to practice, from theology to life. Doctrine is always the basis for duty—duty flows out of doctrine. Doctrine and duty are linked as closely as the flower and the stem, the branch and the trunk, and the trunk and the roots.

The word "therefore" in Ephesians 4:1 indicates the transition—it refers to the doctrine that the subsequent duties are based upon. That was Paul's approach in all his epistles.

A. In Romans

1. Duty

In Romans 12:1 Paul says, "I beseech you therefore, brethren, by the mercies of God, that ye present your bodies a living sacrifice, holy, acceptable unto God, which is your reasonable service." Paul pleaded with the believers at Rome to do their spiritual duty. In verses 3-8 he informs them of the gifts they're to manifest. In verse 9 he tells them about the love they're to manifest. Then he instructs them to be diligent (v. 11), to rejoice (v. 12), to give to the needy (v. 13), to bless their persecutors (v. 14), and to rejoice with those who rejoice and weep with those who weep (v. 15). In chapter 13 he tells them how to respond to the government and to God's standards. Then he teaches them how to respond to a weaker brother (14:1–15:7). In conclusion he discusses how one should carry out his ministry and relate to people in the ministry (15:8–16:27). All of these instructions are practical ones.

2. Doctrine

But the word "therefore" in Romans 12:1 tells us that that practical section is based on the first eleven chapters of theology. Before Paul said anything about what a believer ought to do, he provided eleven chapters of doctrine. Notice in verse 1 he says, "I beseech you therefore, brethren, by the mercies of God." What are the mercies of God? They are the great theological truths he related in the first eleven chapters. On the basis of the great truths God has mercifully extended to us, Paul tells us our duty—our "reasonable service." And that duty is based on the righteousness of God, the uselessness of law and works to achieve salvation, the saving power of faith, peace with God, standing in grace, the promise of glory, the gift of love, the indwelling Spirit, adoption, reconciliation, our union with Christ, deliverance from sin, freedom from judgment, sanctification, justification, glorification, security, and God's unfailing promises. That's why Paul pleads with us to present our bodies to Christ. Duty is always performed in response to doctrine.

B. In Galatians

In the first four chapters of Galatians Paul discusses the liberty of believers—because of Christ we are free from circumcision, free from the Mosaic code, and free from the ceremonial law. None of those things brings about salvation. Paul concludes chapter 4 by saying, "Brethren, we are not children of the bondwoman [Hagar], but of the free [Sarah]" (v. 31). We are free—liberated for life. Immediately following 4:31 is his characteristic "therefore" at the beginning of chapter 5: "It was for freedom that Christ set us free; therefore keep standing firm and do not be subject again to a yoke of slavery" (NASB*). The duty to follow is based on a theology of freedom. Therefore, we are not to be subject to legalism. In chapters 5 and 6 Paul discusses the practical aspects of a life of freedom.

C. In Philippians

In the first chapter Paul taught the Philippians great theological truths about Christ (specifically His consoling character and love) and about what He had done personally in Paul's life. Then Paul said at the beginning of chapter 2, "If there be, therefore, any consolation in Christ, if any comfort of love, if any fellowship of the Spirit, if any tender mercies and compassions, fulfill ye my joy, that ye be likeminded, having the same love, being of one accord, of one mind." Behavior is based on theology.

D. In Colossians

The first two chapters of Colossians contain some of the most exalted presentations of Jesus Christ and the truths of the gospel in Scripture. Chapter 1 is distinguished in its treatment of the glory of Christ (rivaled perhaps by Hebrews 1). In chapter 2 Paul declares that the believer is complete in Christ—he needs nothing more. Beginning in chapter 3 Paul tells us we were risen with Christ who is seated at the right hand of God. Our lives are hidden with Christ in God. When Christ appears we will appear with Him in glory (vv. 1-4). Then in verse 5 he says, "Put to death, therefore, whatever belongs to your earthly nature" (NIV**). From Colossians 1:1–3:4 Paul presents the doctrine, but from 3:5–4:18 he describes the duty.

A Good Kind of Conformity

God expects conformity in the Body of Christ—not conformity to rules and regulations out of fear or legalistic pride, but conformity to righteousness out of deep love and affection for Jesus Christ. We should strongly desire to do what God wants us to do because of all He has done for us. We should walk worthy of Him. A believer

* *New American Standard Bible*
** *New International Version*

is a child of God, a member of God's family—he belongs to the heavenly Father—and that says something about how he ought to live. We disobey God when we fail to live up to His name.

IV. THE PRIORITY OF KNOWLEDGE

We are to walk worthy of our calling, but to do so we must know the principles to follow. In 1 Thessalonians 4:1 Paul says, "We beseech you, brethren, and exhort you by the Lord Jesus, that as ye have received of us how ye ought to walk and please God, so ye would abound more and more." First Paul taught the Thessalonians how to walk and then exhorted them to do it. Instruction must come first—a person can't be expected to function on what he doesn't know. So we must search the Word of God to know the principles of life.

A. The Search for Wisdom

1. Job 28:1-12—Much of this chapter describes the lengths people will go to in order to mine treasures from the earth: "Surely there is a vein for the silver, and a place for gold where they refine it. Iron is taken out of the earth, and bronze is smelted out of the stone. He setteth an end to darkness, and searcheth out all perfection, the stones of darkness, and the shadow of death. . . . The stones of it are the place of sapphires; and it hath dust of gold. There is a path which no fowl knoweth, and which the falcon's eye hath not seen; the lion's whelps have not trodden it, nor the fierce lion passed by it. He putteth forth his hand upon the rock; he overturneth the mountains by the roots. He cutteth out rivers among the rocks; and his eye seeth every precious thing. He bindeth the floods from overflowing" (vv. 1-3, 6-11). Man will do anything to find treasure, but in spite of all his effort he won't find the wisdom of God (v. 12).

2. Proverbs 2:4-6—Solomon says that when you exert as much effort to know the wisdom of God as people exert to find gold and silver, you will know God's wisdom. And until you know God's wisdom, you won't know how to live.

15

3. Colossians 1:9-12—Paul says, "We also, since the day we heard it, do not cease to pray for you, and to desire that ye might be filled with the knowledge of his will in all wisdom and spiritual understanding" (v. 9). The result is in verse 10: "That ye might walk worthy." The worthy walk is predicated on knowledge. So is being fruitful in every good work (v. 10), being strengthened with might (v. 11), and giving thanks (v. 12).

The Danger of Teaching Duty Without Doctrine

I teach the principles of the Word of God so that you can live by them. I could tell stories or appeal to your emotions, but ultimately you'd forget what you heard. Pastors and teachers throughout the church dilute the Word of God when they exhort people about duty without teaching them doctrine. When the principles are removed, the motive to perform the duty is gone.

Let me illustrate it this way: let's assume you drive 55 miles an hour on the highway. The reason you do so is based on a regulation that tells you to drive 55 miles an hour. Your duty is predicated on that regulation. Here is another example: near the first of April you don't suggest to your spouse that you would like to send a large check to the government because it has done so much for you. You don't send it necessarily because you want to; a government regulation requires you to send it.

The Christian life is lived in a similar manner. People don't do things arbitrarily. Unless they know the reason, it is difficult to get them to commit to the duty. Pastors and teachers must teach doctrine. Otherwise they become nothing more than cheerleaders, leading people to commit to things without knowing why.

James 3:1 says, "Be not many teachers, knowing that we shall receive the greater judgment." The Lord will hold me accountable for dispensing His truth to His people. I want to discharge my ministry to the fullest, and that means I must teach you the principles of Scripture. I'm not interested in intimidating you to get you to conform legalistically or emotionally. My responsibility is to teach the Word of God and to allow the Holy Spirit to apply it. If I were to try to whip people into an emotional frenzy or tell them to do things without providing them a theological reason, I would leave them empty. Doctrine is the key to Christian living.

The Key to Church Renewal

There are people in the church who claim that it is more important to show love to people than to teach doctrine. That kind of unbiblical thinking often comes under the heading of church renewal. Several suggestions are typically made regarding how to renew the church. Some think the structure needs to change—eliminate the congregational setting and use small groups to emphasize interaction. But that kind of change often winds up being external and superficial. People can attempt reorganization of the church every six months and still never experience renewal. Why? Because Ephesians 4:23 says, "Be renewed in the spirit of your mind." The church will be renewed only when it teaches God's truth so His people can know it. If that is happening, it matters little how the church structure changes. Once the people are renewed in their minds they will carry on the Lord's work.

B. The Source of Renewal

Church renewal occurs when people's minds are renewed by God's Word.

1. Ephesians 1:17-18—Paul prayed "that the God of our Lord Jesus Christ, the Father of glory, may give unto you the spirit of wisdom and revelation in the knowledge of him, the eyes of your understanding being enlightened." God knows that the heart of renewal is knowledge of His truth.

2. Philippians 1:9-10—Paul prayed "that your love may abound yet more and more in knowledge and in all judgment; that ye may approve things that are excellent." We need to know doctrine and theology or our love will be less than God's love, which is discerning and knowledgeable.

3. Colossians 1:10—Paul again prayed "that ye might walk worthy of the Lord unto all pleasing, being fruitful in every good work, and increasing in the knowledge of God."

4. Colossians 3:10—Paul said, "Put on the new man, that is renewed in knowledge after the image of him that created him."

5. 2 Peter 3:18—Peter said, "Grow in grace, and in the knowledge of our Lord and Savior, Jesus Christ." We need to know the Word of God. We should hunger and search for it as for treasure.

6. Colossians 1:28—Paul wanted everyone to be mature and complete. He described the ministry this way: "warning every man, and teaching every man in all wisdom, that we may present every man perfect in Christ Jesus."

7. 2 Timothy 3:16-17—"All scripture is given by inspiration of God . . . that the man of God may be perfect, thoroughly furnished unto all good works." You need to know God's Word in order to do "all good works."

C. The State of the Church

God expects the church to know His Word. But for many years that has not been its focus. Christians have become so intent on relating to one another that they have forgotten about the foundation of our relationship to one another in the Body of Christ: the Word of God. We need to read and study it more. We can't function effectively within the framework of the church and walk worthy of the Lord Jesus Christ unless we know His standards.

We must strive to know the Word of God, yet realize we can never know enough of it. The apostle Paul knew a great deal, yet the cry of his heart was, "That I may know him" (Phil. 3:10). James desired to "receive . . . the engrafted word" (James 1:21). And Peter said, "As newborn babes, desire the pure milk of the word, that ye might grow by it" (1 Pet. 2:2). God's standard is the basis of our behavior.

18

Conclusion

In Ephesians 4:1 Paul says, "I therefore, the prisoner of the Lord, beseech you that ye walk worthy of the vocation to which ye are called." God calls us to walk worthy of Him. What happens when we do so? Hebrews 11 is a testimony to the great heroes of faith. The first one is Abel, who offered God a more excellent sacrifice than Cain (v. 4). Next is Enoch, who pleased God so much that one day he walked with God into glory—he never died (v. 5). Noah walked with God in faith as he built the ark (v. 7). Abraham and Sarah walked worthy of God (vv. 8-19). Isaac, Jacob, Joseph, and Moses walked with God against all opposition (vv. 20-29). They lived up to what they knew. Even Rahab, the prostitute, walked with God (v. 31). Then the writer of Hebrews said, "What shall I more say? For the time would fail me to tell of Gideon, and of Barak, and of Samson, and of Jephthah, of David also, and Samuel, and of the prophets, who, through faith, subdued kingdoms, wrought righteousness, obtained promises, stopped the mouths of lions, quenched the violence of fire, escaped the edge of the sword, out of weakness were made strong, became valiant in fight, turned to flight the armies of the aliens. Women received their dead raised to life again, and others were tortured, not accepting deliverance, that they might obtain a better resurrection: and others had trial of cruel mockings and scourgings, yea, moreover, of bonds and imprisonment; they were stoned, they were sawn asunder, were tested, were slain with the sword; they wandered about in sheepskins and goatskins; being destitute, afflicted, tormented (of whom the world was not worthy)" (vv. 32-38). If you walk worthy of God, the world is not worthy of you.

Focusing on the Facts

1. What generally happens to someone who doesn't uphold the standards of society (see p. 8)?
2. How can conformity become obsessive with some people? Illustrate that from Scripture (see p. 9).
3. What does the New Testament teach about those who don't conform to biblical standards (see p. 10)?
4. What does Christ expect of us (see p. 11)?
5. What are some of the resources and riches God has given us (see pp. 11-12)?

6. What is the basis for duty (see p. 12)?
7. Give some examples of how doctrine preceded duty in some of Paul's epistles (see pp. 12-14).
8. Where can a believer look to find the principles of life (see p. 15)?
9. According to Colossians 1:9-12, what things are predicated on knowledge (see p. 16)?
10. What happens to the people when their pastors function only like cheerleaders (see p. 16)?
11. What is the only way that church renewal can ever take place (Eph. 4:23; see p. 17)?
12. Give specific examples of believers who walked worthy of God (see pp. 18-19).

Pondering the Principles

1. Review the section that discusses our position in Christ (see pp. 11-12). Ephesians 1-3 delineates many of the blessings God has given us as a result of being in Christ. Read Ephesians 1-3 and record the blessings God has already given us and those He will give us when we are with Christ in heaven. Thank God for everything He has given you. Be especially thankful for the blessings that are most meaningful to you.

2. Read 2 Timothy 3:16-17. What is Scripture able to do for believers? We must search the Bible to know the principles of life. Job 28:1-12 shows to what lengths people will go to recover treasure from the earth. To what lengths do you go to discover the principles that will guide and bless your life? If your goal as a believer is to glorify God and be all that you can for Him, then a practical knowledge of Scripture is essential. Do you read the Bible on a daily basis? Do you understand what you read? How much of what you read do you try to apply every day? To be all that God wants us to be, we need to mine the depths of God's Word and continuously apply what we find to our lives. Examine what that kind of commitment will cost you in time and energy. Be willing to make it.

2
The Lowly Walk—Part 2

Outline

Introduction
A. The Passion of Paul
  1. Acts 26:3
  2. Romans 12:1
  3. 1 Corinthians 4:16
  4. 2 Corinthians 2:8
  5. 2 Corinthians 5:20
  6. Galatians 4:12
B. The Knowledge of God's Word
  1. The protection of knowledge
  2. The peril of knowledge

Lesson
I. The Call to the Worthy Walk (v. 1)
A. The Prisoner (v. 1*a*)
  1. His perspective
  2. His point
B. The Plea (v. 1*b*)
  1. The definition
  2. The display
  3. The desire
C. The Calling (v. 1*c*)
  1. The source of our call
    a) John 6:44
    b) Romans 11:29
    c) Romans 8:30
    d) Ephesians 1:4
    e) John 15:16
    f) 1 Corinthians 1:26
    g) 2 Thessalonians 1:11
    h) 2 Peter 1:10
  2. The response to our call

Conclusion

Introduction

The first three chapters of Ephesians affirm that we have a high position in Christ: we are exalted to heavenly places, blessed with all spiritual blessings, and recipients of the unsearchable riches of Jesus Christ. We are one with Him and citizens of His kingdom. The last three chapters of Ephesians show us how to live in light of who we are.

A. The Passion of Paul

The apostle Paul was passionate when he pleaded with people to know God's Word.

1. Acts 26:3—Paul said to King Agrippa, "I beseech thee to hear me patiently."

2. Romans 12:1—"I beseech you therefore, brethren, by the mercies of God, that ye present your bodies a living sacrifice."

3. 1 Corinthians 4:16—"I beseech you, be ye followers of me."

4. 2 Corinthians 2:8—Paul said regarding an erring brother, "I beseech you that ye would confirm your love toward him."

5. 2 Corinthians 5:20—"We beg you in Christ's stead, be ye reconciled to God."

6. Galatians 4:12—"Brethren, I beseech you, be as I am." In Galatians 5:1 Paul specifies that he had been set free in Christ.

When Paul believed in a vital reality or was committed to some principle of divine truth, he implored people to act.

Intellectual Exercise or Impassioned Preaching?

I can identify with Paul. Sometimes I plead with you, and as a pastor I have every right to do so. I cannot approach the ministry with detachment or indifference.

Some years ago I had an opportunity to speak at one of the major Christian colleges of our land. I was assigned to speak in an expository manner, so I decided upon 1 Corinthians 5 as my text and the motivation of the apostle Paul as my subject. Knowing that the students and faculty were involved in academics all day, I thought they could use some fire and passion. So I poured out my heart to them and preached the best I could. I pleaded with them to respond to the principles of God's Word so that when they left school they would make a difference in the world. After finishing my prayer, I felt as if I had bared my soul to them.

As I walked out of the auditorium, one of the students confronted me. He said, "Apparently you didn't realize to whom you were speaking. You should have been informed as to the intellectual level of the students. Your emotional stories and display were quite unnecessary—in fact, they were offensive. We are mature, intellectual people. Just give us the facts, and we'll judge whether they're relevant to our lives." He didn't understand that a pastor can't do that when his heart is involved in his ministry. I certainly can't detach myself like that. I took his name and later wrote him a note: "Thank you for confronting me, for it makes me think about my ministry. But I must remind you that my ministry is not mere intellectual exercise; I have a deep passion in my heart to see people obey God's Word."

The prophets of God in the Old Testament were passionate men. Jesus Christ Himself was passionate—many times He cried out over the sins of the people. He wept over the city of Jerusalem (Luke 19:41-44). I imagine that tears often streamed down Paul's face, because he wanted the people to respond to God. In Ephesians 4:1 he says, "I therefore, the prisoner of the Lord, beseech you that ye walk worthy of the vocation to which ye are called." He didn't coldly say, "It is essential that you walk worthy"—he begged them. The reason he did so was simple: until you walk worthy, God isn't fully glorified, you aren't fully blessed, the church can't fully function, and the world can't see Jesus Christ.

B. The Knowledge of God's Word

In our last lesson we emphasized the importance of knowing God's truth. There are two important things you need to know in that regard.

1. The protection of knowledge

If you don't know the Word of God you can't protect yourself from sin. The psalmist said, "Thy word have I hidden in mine heart, that I might not sin against thee" (Ps. 119:11). Your defense against sin is the Word of Christ dwelling richly within you (Col. 3:16).

The book of Proverbs is about wisdom, a valuable commodity since where there is ignorance there is usually sin. When you don't know the Word of God you have no defense against sin. Proverbs 7:5-23 illustrates the importance of being protected by God's Word. "Keep . . . from the strange woman, from the foreigner who flattereth with her words. For at the window of my house I looked through my casement [lattice], and beheld among the simple ones [naive people], I discerned among the youths, a young man void of understanding, passing through the street near her corner; and he went the way to her house, in the twilight, in the evening, in the black and dark night. And, behold, there met him a woman with the attire of an harlot, and subtle of heart. (She is loud and stubborn; her feet abide not in her house; now is she outside, now in the streets, and lieth in wait at every corner.) So she caught him, and kissed him, and with an impudent face said unto him, I have peace offerings with me; this day have I paid my vows. Therefore came I forth to meet thee, diligently to seek thy face, and I have found thee. I have decked my bed with coverings of tapestry, with embroidered works, with fine linen of Egypt. I have perfumed my bed with myrrh, aloes, and cinnamon. Come, let us take our fill

24

of love until the morning; let us solace ourselves with love. For my husband is not at home; he is gone on a long journey. He hath taken a bag of money with him, and will come home at the day appointed. With her much fair speech she caused him to yield; with the flattering of her lips she forced him. He goeth after her straightway, as an ox goeth to the slaughter, or as a fool to the correction of the stocks, till an arrow strike through his liver—as a bird hasteneth to the snare, and knoweth not that it is for his life."

To be "void of understanding" is also to be defenseless and vulnerable. Knowing God's truth—knowing it by experience and by application—enables you to say no to sin and yes to righteousness. Anyone who puts his faith in Jesus Christ yet does not keep God's Word constantly at the forefront of his mind will find himself entrapped in sin again and again.

2. The peril of knowledge

Although we must know God's Word in order to defend ourselves against sin and to obey God's will, there is a danger. Once we know His truth, we are held accountable for what we know.

Second Peter 2:21 speaks of apostates—those who knew about Jesus Christ but returned to their former life without ever committing themselves to Him: "It had been better for them not to have known the way of righteousness than, after they have known it, to turn from the holy commandment delivered unto them." It is better never to have known the truth than to turn away from it.

As powerful as that point is, the Lord still commanded us to go into all the world and preach the gospel to every creature (Mark 16:15). Better than knowing the truth and not responding is knowing it so you can respond. Someone could argue that since James 4:17 says, "To him that knoweth to do good, and doeth it not, to him it is sin," it is better not to know the Bible. However, if you don't know the Bible, you never even get the chance to obey it.

Our goal as believers is to know the truth and to obey it. That's how we fulfill God's plan for our lives. The alternative is misery. When you don't know the truth you can't obey it. As a result you'll never know God's blessing. And when you know the truth but don't obey, you'll continually experience the chastening of God.

Paul begged us to walk worthy of Christ. He's our standard. Colossians 3:1-2 says, "If ye, then, be risen with Christ, seek those things which are above, where Christ sitteth on the right hand of God. Set your affections on things above, not things on the earth." Earthly things are to be dead for us (Col. 3:5).

An Exalted Position Demands a Lowly Walk

Is it possible for us to walk worthy? First John 2:6 says, "He that saith he abideth in him [Christ] ought himself to walk, even as he walked." Scripture doesn't ask us to do things we can't do. We can walk worthy by learning God's principles and responding to them. Here's an important point to keep in mind: just because we are exalted with Christ doesn't mean we must live exalted lives. Jesus said, "Take my yoke upon you, and learn of me; for I am meek and lowly in heart" (Matt. 11:29). Our high position demands a lowly walk. Ephesians 4:2-3 says we're to be "with all lowliness and meekness, with long-suffering, forbearing one another in love, endeavoring to keep the unity of the Spirit in the bond of peace."

Lesson

I. THE CALL TO THE WORTHY WALK (v. 1)

The Greek word translated "walk" in Ephesians 4:1 means "daily conduct." The theme of the last three chapters of Ephesians is the believer's conduct: we are to walk in unity (4:1-16), in distinctness (4:17-32), in love (5:1-7), in light (5:8-14), in wisdom (5:15-17), in the Spirit (5:18–6:9), and in preparation for warfare (6:10-24). The Christian walk is embodied in our lifestyle.

The Power of the Worthy Walk

Ephesians 3:16-20 shows that it is possible to walk worthy of Christ. First you must commit yourself to the Holy Spirit and allow Him to strengthen you by His might (v. 16). Then Christ purifies and cleanses you so that He might dwell in you. As He penetrates your life with His love, you are filled with the fullness of God and enabled to do "exceedingly abundantly above all that we ask or think, according to the power that worketh in us" (Eph. 3:20). That's what enables you to walk the worthy walk. You'll never do it by simply knowing theology and trying to live it out on your own. You must commit yourself to the power available through the Holy Spirit before you can walk worthy of your calling as a Christian.

A. The Prisoner (v. 1*a*)

"I therefore, the prisoner of the Lord."

1. His perspective

This is the second time Paul has referred to himself as a prisoner (Eph. 3:1 being the first). He often referred to himself as such (e.g., 2 Tim. 1:8; Philem. 1, 9). Technically he was a prisoner of Rome, but he never saw it that way. That's because he had the ability to see things in light of how they affected Christ. That is the best way to live. We ought to interpret everything with respect to what God's Word says.

No matter what happened in his life, Paul immediately considered how it would affect God. Most people facing difficulties in their lives wonder only how those trials will affect them. That's thinking on an earthly level. But he who has the Word of Christ dwelling in him richly functions within a divine frame of reference. He responds by asking God what He is communicating through the difficulties.

When your mind and heart are committed to God's Word, you will mark every event in your life on the divine grid. A mature Christian is truly God-conscious. David said, "I have set the Lord always before me. . . . Therefore my heart is glad, and my glory rejoiceth" (Ps. 16:8-9). David was happy as long as God was his point of reference.

2. His point

Why did Paul raise for the second time the fact that he was a prisoner? Because he wanted the church to walk worthy of the One who called them, no matter what the cost. In his case the cost was imprisonment—about as bad a circumstance as anyone could endure, especially in ancient times.

The root of the Greek word translated "worthy" speaks of equalizing the scales. A Christian's lifestyle ought to equalize his identity. There ought to be a perfect harmony between who you are and how you live. And your circumstances shouldn't affect that, no matter how bad they might be. The worthy walk may lead to prison and death, as it did for Paul, but it should never impact our commitment to walk worthy of our Lord.

Law vs. Grace

Throughout the Old Testament God told the nation of Israel that if they would obey Him, He would bless them. Blessing was contingent upon obedience. But in the New Testament God tells us that since He has already blessed us with all spiritual blessings in the heavenlies (Eph. 1:3), we ought to obey Him. That's the difference between law and grace. Law says, "If you do this, I'll bless." Grace says, "I've already blessed; now please do this." So we respond to God out of gratitude, not fear.

B. The Plea (v. 1*b*)

"[I] beseech you that ye walk worthy."

28

1. The definition

The Greek word translated "beseech" (*parakaleō*) means "to call to someone with intensity" or "to plead with someone." Paul didn't hesitate to beg people to obey God because he was so concerned about them.

2. The display

Some pastors can put on quite a performance, but that's not how it should be. Ministry is more than preaching a good sermon or creating good programs; it is seeing that people are perfected in Jesus Christ (Col. 1:28). There's never a time that I go home after a day of study or ministry and feel like I have completed my work, because I haven't. A sermon may have been finished, a manuscript may have been written, a problem may have been solved, or a solution to a biblical issue may have been discovered. But I never go home without thinking of the other things that needed to be done, like talking to a certain person, helping someone, calling someone, writing someone, or taking care of a family that needs help. Truly a pastor's work is never done.

I know what Paul meant when he said, "Beside those things that are without [his physical suffering], that which cometh upon me daily, the care of all the churches" (2 Cor. 11:28). To see the saints become mature is the goal that drives the pastor. Paul said, "We preach, warning every man, and teaching every man in all wisdom, that we may present every man perfect [mature, complete] in Christ Jesus" (Col. 1:28). In Galatians 4:19 he says, "My little children, of whom I travail in birth again until Christ be formed in you." The growth of the saints was his great desire.

3. The desire

Spiritual maturity is the goal of ministry. Paul was so committed to that goal that he prayed night and day for it to be a reality in the lives of the people (1 Thess. 3:10). The servant of God gives his life for the spiritual maturity of the flock. If a minister is ever satisfied with anything less, he ought to get out of the ministry.

C. The Calling (v. 1c)

"Of the vocation [calling] to which ye are called."

Your lifestyle should match your calling. First let us consider who called you to Christ.

1. The source of our call

   a) John 6:44—Jesus said, "No man can come to me, except the Father, who hath sent me, draw him."

   b) Romans 11:29—"The gifts and calling of God are without repentance."

   c) Romans 8:30—"Whom he did predestinate, them he also called; and whom he called, them he also justified; and whom he justified, them he also glorified." God called you.

   d) Ephesians 1:4—"He hath chosen us in him before the foundation of the world."

   e) John 15:16—Jesus said to His disciples, "Ye have not chosen me, but I have chosen you and ordained you."

   f) 1 Corinthians 1:26—Paul said, "Ye see your calling, brethren, how that not many wise men, not many mighty, not many noble, are called."

   g) 2 Thessalonians 1:11—Paul said, "We pray always for you, that our God would count you worthy of this calling."

   h) 2 Peter 1:10—"Give diligence to make your calling and election sure."

2. The response to our call

   Suppose after investigating all the different religions of the world, a person chose Christianity. If Christianity was nothing more than a simple, personal choice to be saved, the person would have a certain level of commitment to it. The thinking would be, *Since I have decided to do it, it's worth doing.* However, the knowledge that you are a Christian because the sovereign, almighty ruler of the universe wrote your name in a book before the world began creates a much higher level of commitment.

Suppose a single woman approached a young bachelor, told him he had characteristics she admired, and asked him if he would be interested in marrying her; and suppose he agreed. Obviously there would be something missing in that courtship. But suppose the young bachelor approached this young woman first and told her she was the loveliest girl he had ever seen, and that he had gone from one end of the world to the other and had found that her beauty and character surpassed all others. When he asks her for her hand in marriage we know that nothing is missing.

Magnify that illustration to God's perspective. We didn't ask God if we could get in on a salvation deal. No. Out of all the world He chose us—and that's a high calling (Phil. 3:14). It's also a holy calling (2 Tim. 1:9) and a heavenly calling (Heb. 3:1). Such a calling demands a response.

Conclusion

Only one thing matters from the moment you become a Christian until the day you see Jesus—that you walk worthy and live up to who you are in Him. What you own, what you know, and what you do for a living are not all that important. Neither is how often you come to church. What matters is that you walk worthy of Christ on a moment-by-moment basis.

Suppose that immediately after you were saved, the Lord stamped your forehead with the words, "Watch me. I'm a child of God." What would that do to your lifestyle? If I love God and Christ, it will make a big change. Inasmuch as we wear the name of Jesus Christ, shouldn't we walk worthy of it? Inasmuch as we possess all the blessings of the Savior, shouldn't we live up to them? God has blessed us and wants us to obey Him. I beg you to walk worthy of Him!

31

Focusing on the Facts

1. Describe the passion of Paul (p. 22).
2. Why did Paul entreat people to walk worthy of their calling (see p. 24)?
3. What is the believer's defense against sin (Col. 3:16; see p. 24)?
4. Why is there an element of danger in knowledge (see p. 25)?
5. Explain the reasoning of 2 Peter 2:21 (see p. 25).
6. How can we reconcile that reasoning with Christ's command in Mark 16:15 (see p. 25)?
7. What should be our goal as Christians (see p. 26)?
8. What does our high position in Christ demand from us (Eph. 4:2-3; see p. 26)?
9. What does the Greek word translated "walk" mean (see p. 26)?
10. How is it possible for a Christian to walk worthy of his calling (Eph. 3:16-20; see p. 27)?
11. Although Paul was technically a prisoner of Rome, why did he call himself a prisoner of Christ (see p. 27)?
12. How does a mature Christian view the trials in his life (see pp. 27-28)?
13. To what does the Greek word translated "worthy" refer? How does that apply to a Christian's lifestyle (see p. 28)?
14. Explain the difference between law and grace in terms of our calling (see p. 28).
15. Define the Greek word translated "beseech" (see p. 29).
16. Explain the difference between your choosing salvation and God's choosing to save you (see pp. 30-31).

Pondering the Principles

1. The believer's best defense against sin is knowing and applying God's Word. One of the most important passages in Scripture about the excellency of God's Word is Psalm 119. Read the entire psalm. Record every occasion where the psalmist says that God's Word is effective in dealing with sin. What is your responsibility in each case? What is God's responsibility? Begin to apply God's Word to the sins you struggle with most. Memorize verse 11 and make it the prayer of your heart: "Thy word I have treasured in my heart, that I may not sin against Thee" (NASB).

2. As believers we ought to look at everything and every event from God's perspective. When any trial or opportunity comes our way, we need to seek God's wisdom in how to handle it. We also need to have God's perspective on the things we possess: do we look at them as things God has given us stewardship of, or do we see them as things we have attained on our own? How do you presently look at trials? Life's decisions? Possessions? Read James 1:2-12 for the biblical perspective on trials. Read Proverbs 3:5-7 for God's perspective on life's decisions. Also read Matthew 6:19-21 and 1 Timothy 6:5-11, 17-19 for the biblical perspective on riches and possessions. Make it your goal to see everything in your life from God's perspective.

3
The Lowly Walk—Part 3

Outline

Introduction
A. A General Analysis
   1. The standard of humility
   2. The exaltation of pride
B. A Biblical Analysis
   1. On pride
      a) Proverbial injunctions
         (1) Proverbs 11:2
         (2) Proverbs 16:5
         (3) Proverbs 16:18
         (4) Proverbs 21:4
      b) Biblical perspectives
         (1) Isaiah 2:10-17
         (2) Isaiah 3:16-25
         (3) Jeremiah 50:31-32
         (4) Malachi 4:1
         (5) James 4:6
         (6) 1 John 2:16-17
   2. On humility
      a) A virtue of righteousness
         (1) Proverbs 15:33
         (2) Proverbs 22:4
         (3) Proverbs 27:2
      b) An ingredient for blessing
      c) The standard of salvation
         (1) Matthew 18:3-4
         (2) Luke 18:13-14

Review
I. The Call to the Worthy Walk (v. 1)

Lesson
II. The Characteristics of the Lowly Walk (vv. 2-3)
 A. Humility
  1. The meaning of humility
   a) Its positive definition
   b) Its negative definition
  2. The models of humility
   a) Jesus
   b) Paul
   c) John the Baptist
   d) Mary (Martha's sister)
   e) The writers of the gospels
    (1) Matthew
    (2) Mark
    (3) John
  3. The manifestation of humility
   a) Self-awareness
    (1) Regularly confessing our sins
    (2) Not comparing ourselves to others
   b) Christ-awareness
   c) God-awareness

Introduction

Walking worthy refers to living a life that matches your position in Christ. The first three chapters of Ephesians discuss the believer's position in Christ; the last three discuss his practice. The Greek word translated "worthy" in Ephesians 4:1 refers to balance—to equalizing a scale. It is our duty as Christians to equalize our behavior with our identity.

How do we walk worthy? Ephesians 4:2-3 says, "With all lowliness and meekness, with long-suffering, forbearing one another in love, endeavoring to keep the unity of the Spirit in the bond of peace." The five characteristics of the worthy walk are humility, meekness, patience, love, and unity. Humility is the all-inclusive principle. Yet although those characteristics belong together—like synonyms—they are also different. There is a progression involved:

humility leads to meekness, which leads to patience, which leads to love, which finally leads to unity.

A. A General Analysis

1. The standard of humility

Humility is an elusive quality—the moment you think you are humble is just when you forfeit it. Yet humility is essential. It is at the heart of the worthy walk.

Jesus came into the world as the King of Kings and Lord of Lords, exalted above any human who has ever lived or ever will live. Yet the apostle Paul said that He humbled Himself by taking on the form of a servant (Phil. 2:7). In Matthew 11:29 Jesus says, "I am meek and lowly in heart." He was born in a stable. He never had a place of His own to lay His head. He possessed no property; He owned only the garments on His body. He was buried in a borrowed tomb. His only home was the Mount of Olives, where He would retire in the evening in solitude to commune with the Father.

Jesus set the standard for us. First John 2:6 says, "He that saith he abideth in him ought himself also so to walk, even as he walked." Since He walked in humility, that's the way we are to walk.

2. The exaltation of pride

Humility is foreign to our world because our world exalts pride. Our society, as well as others throughout history, tends to view humility as a weakness, an infirmity, something ignoble to be despised. The world views a humble person as the proverbial Caspar Milquetoast, who is afraid of his own shadow.

People in our society love to talk about things of which they are proud. Indeed ours is an ostentatious, boastful, demanding, self-exalting society.

B. A Biblical Analysis

1. On pride

Pride was the first sin. It was committed by the angel Lucifer, who decided to exalt himself above God (Isa. 14:12-15; Ezek. 28:11-19).

a) Proverbial injunctions

(1) Proverbs 11:2—"When pride cometh, then cometh shame; but with the lowly is wisdom."

(2) Proverbs 16:5—"Every one who is proud in heart is an abomination to the Lord."

(3) Proverbs 16:18—"Pride goeth before destruction, and an haughty spirit before a fall."

(4) Proverbs 21:4—"An high look [the external manifestation of pride] and a proud heart [the internal manifestation of pride] . . . are sin."

Humility is the virtue of the righteous; pride is the sin of the unrighteous. It should grieve the soul of any Christian to see himself or a brother in Christ exalt pride. I'll never forget a meeting I had at my home some years ago with some seminary students. One of the students asked in a very serious tone, "How did you finally overcome pride?" I hated to disappoint him, but I have not overcome pride! That's a lifetime battle for every Christian. Satan keeps fighting us on that front all the time.

b) Biblical perspectives

(1) Isaiah 2:10-17—"Enter into the rock, and hide in the dust, for fear of the Lord, and for the glory of his majesty" (v. 10). When you start comparing yourself with God, you'd better get under a rock, because you can't compare to the majesty of God. Isaiah continues, "The lofty looks of man shall be humbled, and the haughtiness of men shall be bowed down, and the Lord alone shall be exalted

in that day" (v. 11). Pride is sin because in essence it's competing with God. Pride leads you to exalt yourself and diminish God's glory. But God will not give His glory to another—He alone is worthy of exaltation. We're exalted only because He chooses to elevate us.

In verses 12-17 Isaiah chooses a series of metaphors to refer to the destiny of the proud: "The day of the Lord of hosts shall be upon every one who is proud and lofty, and upon every one who is lifted up, and he shall be brought low; and upon all the cedars of Lebanon, that are high and lifted up, and upon all the oaks of Bashan, and upon all the high mountains, and upon all the hills that are lifted up, and upon every high tower, and upon every fortified wall, and upon all the ships of Tarshish, and upon all pleasant pictures. And the loftiness of man shall be bowed down, and the haughtiness of men shall be made low; and the Lord alone shall be exalted in that day." God will judge the proud.

A Parade of Pride

The people in Isaiah's day paraded their pride, much like our society does. We want the fanciest clothes, the best car, the nicest house—the best of everything. Often that's because we want to be better than someone else. Of course we have certain needs, but there's a fine line between what we need and what we want. When our needs are overruled by our wants and we desire something better purely for the sake of self-exaltation and self-gratification, that's pride on display. As we acquire more things and reach a certain level of prosperity, we can begin to despise those beneath our level and aspire to those above us. That is another step of pride.

(2) Isaiah 3:16-25—"The Lord saith, Because the daughters of Zion are haughty, and walk with stretched forth necks and wanton eyes, walking and mincing as they go, and making a tinkling with their feet; therefore the Lord will smite with a scab the crown of the head of the daughters of

39

Zion, and the Lord will uncover their secret parts. In that day the Lord will take away the bravery of their tinkling anklets, and their headbands, and their crescents like the moon, the pendants, and the bracelets, and the veils, the headdresses, and the armlets, and the sashes, and the perfume boxes, and the amulets, the rings, and nose rings, the festival robes, and the mantles, and the cloaks, and the handbags, the hand mirrors, and the linen wrappers, and the turbans, and the veils. And it shall come to pass, that instead of sweet fragrance there shall be rottenness; and instead of a girdle, a rope; and instead of well set hair, baldness; and instead of a robe, a girding of sackcloth; and branding instead of beauty. Thy men shall fall by the sword." That society was made up of show-offs. They exalted themselves to attract attention when they should have been acting as instruments to point people to God.

(3) Jeremiah 50:31-32—"Behold, I am against thee, O thou most proud, saith the Lord God of hosts; for thy day is come, the time that I will punish thee. And the most proud shall stumble and fall, and none shall raise him up; and I will kindle a fire in his cities, and it shall devour all round about him."

(4) Malachi 4:1—"The day cometh, that shall burn like an oven, and all the proud, yea, and all that do wickedly, shall be stubble; and the day that cometh shall burn them up, saith the Lord of hosts, that it shall leave them neither root nor branch."

(5) James 4:6—"God resisteth the proud, but giveth grace unto the humble" (cf. Prov. 3:34).

(6) 1 John 2:16-17—"All that is in the world, the lust of the flesh, and the lust of the eyes, and the pride of life, is not of the Father, but is of the world. And the world passeth away, and the lust of it."

2. On humility

   a) A virtue of righteousness

   God is for humility as strongly as He is against pride. Humility is the virtue of the righteous.

   (1) Proverbs 15:33—"Before honor is humility."

   (2) Proverbs 22:4—"By humility and the fear of the Lord are riches, honor, and life."

   (3) Proverbs 27:2—"Let another man praise thee, and not thine own mouth."

What to Do When You're Feeling Proud

When you begin to feel proud of yourself, read the following verses:

1. Isaiah 51:1—"Look unto the rock from which ye are hewn, and to the hole of the pit from which ye are digged." Remember where you came from before you were saved.

2. Ephesians 2:1-3—"[You] were dead in trespasses and sins; in which times past ye walked according to the course of this world, according to the prince of the power of the air, the spirit that now worketh in the sons of disobedience; among whom also we all had our manner of life in times past in the lusts of our flesh, fulfilling the desires of the flesh and of the mind, and were by nature the children of wrath."

   b) An ingredient for blessing

   Humility is a basic ingredient necessary for all spiritual blessing. God will bless only the humble. We forget how important humility is, but every sin has its root in pride. All sin is defiance of God and His holiness. We so often grapple with the peripheral issues instead of dealing with our pride. For example, the Christian family struggles with all sorts of problems in our day. So often Dad, Mom, and the kids seek methods to patch up the external problems while the primary problem—pride among the family members—is ignored. But there will never be unity, honor, happiness, or graciousness in the family until first there is humility. It doesn't matter if you have served the Lord in great ways, because if you're not walking in humility, you won't know how to walk worthy of Christ. The worthy walk begins with humility.

c) The standard of salvation

There is no salvation apart from humility.

(1) Matthew 18:3-4—Jesus said, "Except ye be converted, and become as little children, ye shall not enter into the kingdom of heaven. Whosoever, therefore, shall humble himself as this little child, the same is greatest in the kingdom of heaven." Until a person comes to God and confesses that he is a sinner worthy of nothing, he can't be saved. You can't approach God and tell Him you deserve to be in heaven because you have honors and degrees; you must approach Him in humility as a sinner. There's no other way to get into the family of God, and there's no other way to live once you're there.

(2) Luke 18:13-14—Jesus said, "The tax collector, standing afar off, would not lift so much as his eyes unto heaven, but smote upon his breast, saying, God be merciful to me a sinner. I tell you, this man went down to his house justified rather than the other; for everyone that exalteth himself shall be abased; and he that humbleth himself shall be exalted."

Review

I. THE CALL TO THE WORTHY WALK (v. 1; see pp. 26-31)

Lesson

II. THE CHARACTERISTICS OF THE LOWLY WALK (vv. 2-3)

"With all lowliness and meekness, with long-suffering, forbearing one another in love, endeavoring to keep the unity of the Spirit in the bond of peace."

Why Is Unity in the Church So Important?

The unity of believers is critical. Paul emphasized that point in the first three chapters of Ephesians: we are one new man (2:14), one body (2:16), one household (2:19), and one habitation of the Spirit (2:22). Both Jew and Gentile are one in Christ. We know unity is important because of Christ's prayer: "That they all may be one, as thou, Father, art in me, and I in thee, that they also may be one in us; that the world may believe that thou hast sent me. . . . I in them, and thou in me, that they be made perfect in one; and that the world may know that thou hast sent me" (John 17:21, 23). When we are united, we manifest Christ to the world.

The world is full of discord, animosity, bitterness, and resentment. It exalts rugged individualism—the idea of every man for himself. If in the midst of that discord is an oasis of people unified in peace, the world will stop and wonder what causes it. That unity would give us the perfect platform to proclaim Jesus Christ because only He can produce that kind of peace.

Every peace treaty that's been made throughout world history has eventually been broken. The Bible says there is no peace for the wicked (Isa. 57:21). People cry for peace, but there is no peace (Jer. 8:11). No one in the world has ever been able to achieve peace. That's why the nations will gravitate toward the Antichrist. He will first appear as a great peacemaker. But we can show that Christ is the true peacemaker if we are a community of peaceful, loving, united people. The heart of our testimony to the world is that Christ was sent from God because only God can make true, lasting peace.

A. Humility

1. The meaning of humility

a) Its positive definition

The Greek word translated "all" (*pasa*) in the phrase "all lowliness" means "total." So Paul was speaking of total humility. We are to manifest humility in everything—in every relationship, in every attitude, and in every deed.

The Greek word translated "lowliness" (*tapeinophrosunē*) is a compound word. It comes from two Greek words: *tapeinos* and *phroneō*. *Tapeinos* means "low" as opposed to high.

It also has a metaphorical use, sometimes referring to poor people, or cowardly persons, or unimportant priorities. *Phroneō* means "to think" or "to judge." The combination of the two means we are to think of ourselves as poor and of low priority.

Paul said that a person should not "think of himself more highly than he ought to think" (Rom. 12:3). We're to have a humble estimation of ourselves. But our society constantly tells us to think highly of ourselves—to be proud. Clearly that contradicts what the Bible says.

b) Its negative definition

Tapeinophrosunē never appears in classical Greek because it was basically coined by Christians. The Greeks and Romans ascribed no virtue to humility and even failed to acknowledge it. They despised the attitude. Even after the Christians developed the term to refer to humility as a virtue, the pagans couldn't reconcile it with their views. So every time *tapeinophrosunē* appeared in their first or second-century writings, it was used in a derogatory manner to refer to anyone who was weak, cowardly, and fainthearted.

It grieves me to hear so-called ministers preach that Christians need to think of themselves as great. That's not what the Bible teaches. Unbelievers may continue to look at humility as a pitiable weakness. But in Christ, humility becomes a beautiful virtue. Without it no one can walk worthy of Him.

2. The models of humility

a) Jesus

Jesus is the perfect model of humility. He was acquainted with grief (Matt. 26:38). He gave of Himself (John 6:51). He was hated without cause (John 15:18, 25). He was homeless (Matt. 8:20), persecuted (John 15:20), betrayed (Matt. 26:23-25), condemned and delivered up (Matt. 20:18), despised (Luke 18:32), lifted up on a cross (John 12:32-34), mocked (Mark 10:34), numbered with criminals (Luke 22:37), and killed (Matt. 16:21). Christ was indeed humble, and we must walk as He walked.

Becoming a Slave to Save a Slave

When the evangelical Moravian Brethren of Germany heard about slavery in the West Indies, they were told it was impossible to reach the slave population without first becoming a slave. Two men volunteered and began their journey in 1732. If necessary they would volunteer to receive lashes to get beside the slaves and teach them about Christ. The other slaves listened to them because they were touched by the men's willingness to be humbled. While that is a glorious example, Christ's example is infinitely greater. He humbled Himself and became one of us. He embraced us and drew us to Him, though we were once slaves of sin.

Even though Jesus was God, He walked in humility. And even though we're special in God's eyes, we're to walk humbly as well. Psalm 138:6 says, "Though the Lord be high, yet hath he respect unto the lowly." May God preserve us from ever exalting ourselves and looking down on others.

b) Paul

In Acts 20:19 Paul says he was "serving the Lord with all humility of mind, and with many tears, and trials." If you don't have a servant's heart you'll never walk worthy of the Master. We're to be *hupēretēs*—literally "under-rowers," originally indicating the lowest galley slaves, the ones rowing on the bottom tier of a ship (1 Cor. 4:1).

Paul boasted in only one thing: the gospel of Jesus Christ (2 Cor. 10:8-18). He said, "By the grace of God I am what I am" (1 Cor. 15:10). Paul recognized that although he had been a blasphemer and a persecutor—the chief of sinners—God counted him faithful and put him into the ministry (1 Tim. 1:12-15).

c) John the Baptist

Of John the Baptist Jesus said, "Among them that are born of women there hath not risen a greater than John the Baptist" (Matt. 11:11). Jesus called him the greatest man who ever lived. Yet John the Baptist said, "He [Christ] must increase, but I must decrease" (John 3:30). He also said he wasn't worthy even to loosen Christ's shoe (John 1:27).

d) Mary (Martha's sister)

On three occasions the Bible tells of Mary being beside Jesus' feet (Luke 10:39; John 11:32; 12:3). On one of those occasions Martha was busy preparing for a great meal, and she was upset at Mary for not helping. But Jesus told Martha that she had the wrong priority (Luke 10:38-42).

e) The writers of the gospels

The gospel writers could have elevated themselves after having been with Jesus. Yet the opposite is true—it's almost as if they attempted to hide their identities in their narratives.

(1) Matthew

Matthew was the only author who introduced himself in his gospel, but he did so indirectly (Matt. 9:9)—he didn't mention that it was he who hosted the tremendous feast to introduce tax collectors and sinners to Jesus (cf. Luke 5:27-35).

(2) Mark

Mark, writing under the tutelage of Peter, reflected Peter's perspective. Yet Mark did not include two of the greatest things that ever happened to Peter: his walking on water (Matt. 14:29-33) and his receiving the keys to the kingdom (Matt. 16:19). But Peter's rebuke by Christ (Mark 8:33) and his fall (Mark 14:66-72) are faithfully recorded.

(3) John

John wrote a twenty-one chapter gospel and never once mentioned his own name.

3. The manifestation of humility

a) Self-awareness

Humility begins with self-awareness. The twelfth-century monk Bernard of Clairvaux wrote a book on humility and pride. In it he defined humility as the virtue by which a man becomes conscious of his own unworthiness. Humility starts with looking at ourselves honestly. I believe that involves:

(1) Regularly confessing our sins

You can mask who you really are. You can convince yourself you're something wonderful and never be honest with yourself. But 1 John 1:9 and James 5:16 say that believers are to be constantly confessing their sins. We are to be like Paul, who said he was the chief of sinners (1 Tim. 1:15). We are to press toward the mark of Jesus' high calling, while realizing that we haven't attained it (Phil. 3:12-14). Whenever we're tempted to be proud, we need to remember who we are.

(2) Not comparing ourselves to others

We often become confused about who we really are when we compare ourselves with other people. We can always find someone worse off and say to ourselves, *I'm not so bad; look at him!* I used to use that technique on my mother. She was always concerned about my grades in school. She would be upset when I got a C, and I would say, "But mom, ten kids got a D." You can always find someone with a lower standard. The same thing is true in the home. A wife nags her husband, so he tells her to marry the drunk who lives next door. You can always find someone to make you look good by comparison.

However, you must deal with yourself honestly before God. Paul gives us the principle in 2 Corinthians 10:12: "We dare not make ourselves of the number, or compare ourselves with some that commend themselves; but they, measuring themselves by themselves, and comparing themselves among themselves, are not wise." If we're to be honest with ourselves and with God, we need to evaluate ourselves by outside standards. Humility starts when we take off the rose-colored glasses of self-love so that we can see that we're nothing but unworthy sinners. We need to recognize our faults and confess our sins daily.

b) Christ-awareness

Jesus Christ is our standard. We need to compare ourselves to Him, not to our own standards. First John 2:6 says, "He that saith he abideth in him ought himself also so to walk, even as he walked."

As you look at Jesus Christ in His humanness, you see Him as a perfect man. Then you should feel inadequate. He said the perfect words at the perfect time, and He had the perfect attitude for every situation. He knew how to help in just the perfect way everyone who needed help. What a standard He set!

c) God-awareness

When you look beyond Christ's humanity, you clearly see His deity. And when you compare yourself to God, you realize you are very small.

My Most Humiliating Experience

Often I've been asked, "What is the most humiliating experience you've ever had?" Usually people think of something embarrassing. But the most truly humbling experience I ever had was preaching the gospel of John. It took two years to preach—eighty-eight sermons of about one hundred hours of preaching and somewhere between two and three thousand hours of study. As I studied that gospel week after week, I was constantly faced with the deity of Jesus Christ. Living with the deity of Christ day after day and comparing yourself constantly to Him is one of the healthiest—and most humbling—things you can ever do.

When the prophet Isaiah had the opportunity to see God, he was struck by his own sinfulness in comparison: "In the year that King Uzziah died, I saw also the Lord sitting upon a throne, high and lifted up, and his train filled the temple. Above it stood the seraphim: each one had six wings; with two he covered his face, and with two he covered his feet, and with two he did fly. And one cried unto another, and said, Holy, holy, holy, is the Lord of hosts; the whole earth is full of his glory. And the posts of the door moved at the voice of him who cried, and the house was filled with smoke. Then said I, Woe is me! For I am undone, because I am a man of unclean lips, and I dwell in the midst of a people of unclean lips; for mine eyes have seen the King, the Lord of hosts" (Isa. 6:1-5).

When Paul saw himself for who he really was, he said he was the chief of sinners. That's a proper self-awareness. When Peter saw Jesus he said, "Depart from me; for I am a sinful man, O Lord" (Luke 5:8). That's a proper Christ-awareness. When Isaiah saw God he said, "Woe is me . . . because I am a man of unclean lips" (Isa. 6:5). That's a proper God-awareness. When we see God we should say, "What is man, that thou art mindful of him? And the son of man, that thou visitest him?" (Ps. 8:4). If we all would be so humble, we would have an incredible testimony in the world.

Focusing on the Facts

1. What are the five characteristics of the worthy walk (Eph. 4:2-3; see pp. 36-37)?
2. Who set the standard of humility? Explain (see p. 37).
3. Why is humility a characteristic foreign to our world (see p. 37)?
4. What was the first sin? Who committed it (see p. 38)?
5. Humility is the _____ of the _____ ; pride is the _____ of the _____ (see p. 38).
6. What is the essence of pride (see p. 39)?
7. What tends to happen when people acquire many possessions (see p. 39)?

8. What attitude must people have before they can be saved (Matt. 18:3-4; see p. 42)?
9. Why is unity in the church so important (see pp. 43-44)?
10. Define the Greek phrase translated "all lowliness" in Ephesians 4:2 (see p. 44).
11. Why didn't the Greeks or the Romans have a word for humility (see p. 45)?
12. In what ways was Jesus a model of humility (see p. 45)?
13. Name some others who were models of humility. In what ways did they manifest humility (see pp. 46-47)?
14. How does humility begin? What does it involve? Explain (see pp. 48-49).
15. How do Christ's humanity and deity serve as our standards (see p. 49)?

Pondering the Principles

1. Pride can be defined as the sin of competing against God by exalting ourselves and thus trying to steal His glory. In what specific ways are you guilty of pride? According to James 4:6, what happens when you try to exalt yourself? What happens when you don't? As a reminder, memorize Proverbs 22:4 and commit yourself to glorifying God.

2. In John 17:21, 23 Jesus prayed for unity among believers. In that case Jesus asked God to make us one. But what responsibility do we have? Read Ephesians 4:3 and Hebrews 10:24-25. Are you fulfilling your role in manifesting Christ to the world through the corporate testimony of the church? In what ways are you hindering that testimony? If you need to make peace with a brother or sister in Christ, do so now (Matt. 5:21-24). As long as you don't, some people in this world are acquiring a distorted view of Christianity.

3. To start on the road to humility, you need to follow the steps outlined on pages 48-49. Begin by taking a long, hard look at yourself. Where are you struggling with pride? Be honest. Ask God to reveal any other areas to you that you can't clearly see now. Begin to confess those things daily. As you recognize other sins, confess them as well. Make this procedure a daily practice in your life. To help solidify your confession and to help you see your daily need for it, begin comparing yourself to

Christ. Make a record of the passages in Scripture that discuss either the humanity or the deity of Christ. From then on, whenever you examine your life for sin, read those passages. As you do that on a consistent basis, you'll begin to develop a humble attitude.

4
The Lowly Walk—Part 4

Outline

Introduction

Review
 I. The Call to the Lowly Walk (v. 1)
 II. The Characteristics of the Lowly Walk (vv. 2-3)
 A. Humility
   1. The meaning of humility
   2. The models of humility
   3. The manifestation of humility
     a) Self-awareness
     b) Christ-awareness
     c) God-awareness

Lesson
   4. The menace to humility
     a) Pride in one's abilities
       (1) Identified
       (2) Illustrated
         (*a*) Paul's education
         (*b*) Paul's personality
     b) Pride in one's economic status
       (1) Deuteronomy 8:11-20
       (2) Isaiah 5:8
       (3) Revelation 3:17
     c) Pride in one's deeds
       (1) Bragging about what we have done
       (2) Bragging about what we're going to do

Introduction

When Jesus began His ministry His first message was, "Repent; for the kingdom of heaven is at hand" (Matt. 4:17). Once He gathered believers about Him, He needed to instruct them on how to live as subjects of the kingdom. That's what Matthew 5:1-12 is all about: "Seeing the multitudes, he went up into a mountain: and when he was seated, his disciples came unto him. And he opened his mouth, and taught them, saying, Blessed are the poor in spirit; for theirs is the kingdom of heaven. Blessed are they that mourn; for they shall be comforted. Blessed are the meek; for they shall inherit the earth. Blessed are they who do hunger and thirst after righteousness; for they shall be filled. Blessed are the merciful; for they shall obtain mercy. Blessed are the pure in heart; for they shall see God. Blessed are the peacemakers; for they shall be called the sons of God. Blessed are they who are persecuted for righteousness' sake; for theirs is the kingdom of heaven. Blessed are ye, when men shall revile you, and persecute you, and shall say all manner of evil against you falsely, for my sake. Rejoice, and be exceedingly glad; for great is your reward in heaven; for so persecuted they the prophets who were before you."

We live in a society that denigrates the virtues of Matthew 5:1-12. But according to Jesus, those virtues are to be characteristic of the people in His kingdom.

Review

I. THE CALL TO THE LOWLY WALK (v. 1; see pp. 26-31)

II. THE CHARACTERISTICS OF THE LOWLY WALK (vv. 2-3)

"With all lowliness and meekness, with long-suffering, forbearing one another in love, endeavoring to keep the unity of the Spirit in the bond of peace."

A. Humility

First Peter 5:5 addresses those in the pastorate—those who would receive the recognition, honor, and love of the flock: "Be clothed with humility; for God resisteth the proud, and giveth grace to the humble." The Greek word translated "clothed" referred to the apron worn by a laborer to prevent his clothes from getting soiled. Peter was saying that spiritual leaders need to cover up all the honor and recognition they receive with a humble attitude.

1. The meaning of humility (see pp. 44-45)

2. The models of humility (see pp. 45-47)

3. The manifestation of humility (see pp. 48-49)

   a) Self-awareness (see p. 48)

   b) Christ-awareness (see p. 49)

   c) God-awareness (see p. 49)

When we are honest enough to see our sinfulness, when we see the majesty of Jesus Christ, and when we know what God is like, we will be humble. We'll never become humble by sitting in a corner wishing we were. But we can become humble by sitting in that same corner and confessing our sins, failures, and inadequacies to God. We'll gain humility when we open the pages of God's Word and see the majesty of God and Jesus Christ.

God Himself inevitably helps us along the path to humility. Paul said he had had so many visions and revelations that the Lord gave him a thorn in the flesh to keep him humble (2 Cor. 12:7). The Lord may put something in your life to cause you to see yourself for who you really are. It may be a person you can't handle, a problem you can't solve, or a physical ailment you can't overcome. But the purpose of those things will be to help you maintain a proper understanding of who you are and who God is.

Lesson

4. The menace to humility

What tempts us to be proud? On what battlefields do we fight to be humble? In what areas does Satan tempt us?

a) Pride in one's abilities

(1) Identified

We are often tempted to be proud of our strengths. For example, I've never been tempted to be proud about my fantastic mathematical ability because I don't have any. I've never been tempted to boast about my tremendous musical expertise—the best I can do is sing the melody line. But I am tempted to be proud of my preaching ability because God has given it to me as a gift. If I give in to that temptation, during the week I inevitably get a letter from someone who says something like, "I was in your church Sunday, and I want you to know that I violently disagree with

56

everything you said. I brought my neighbor and you offended her. I'm never coming back again!" Someone said to me on one occasion, "We came to hear you for the first time, but we like our pastor better." Times like those help me keep the proper perspective.

(2) Illustrated

(a) Paul's education

Paul was a well-educated man. He studied at the feet of Gamaliel, a religious authority; was trained in the rabbinic traditions; and knew the Old Testament very well. He had a philosophical mind. Yet in 1 Corinthians 2:1-2 he says, "When I came to you, [I] came not with excellency of speech or of wisdom, declaring unto you the testimony of God. For I determined not to know any thing among you, except Jesus Christ, and him crucified." Paul didn't manipulate his listeners with his intellect and philosophy.

(b) Paul's personality

Paul also had a dynamic personality. He was an intense, fiery, courageous individual. He had to have been, considering at one time his goal in life was to exterminate the Christian faith. He had been a spiritual bounty hunter. With that background he could have approached his ministry with the tact of a bulldog. But in 1 Corinthians 2:3-5 he says, "I was with you in weakness, and in fear, and in much trembling. And my speech and my preaching were not with enticing words of man's wisdom, but in demonstration of the Spirit and of power; that your faith should not stand in the wisdom of men, but in the power of God."

Paul avoided the temptation to turn his strengths into sin. He didn't abuse his power of personality,

57

his ability to communicate, his logic, and his knowledge of philosophy. Later, in 2 Corinthians 12:10, he says, "I take pleasure in infirmities . . . for when I am weak, then am I strong." We're all tempted to abuse our strengths by flaunting them. We like to let people know about the things we do well. It's difficult to stay humble about those things. But the key is to remember that whatever you do well is because God first gave you the ability. Any talent useful to God is a gift of the Holy Spirit. All the credit belongs to Him.

b) Pride in one's economic status

If I were to preach about this temptation in some parts of the world, the people wouldn't understand what I was talking about. People who live in homes with mud floors, walls, and roofs wouldn't be able to relate. But in America, economic pride is a big problem. People boast about their riches. They trust in them. And they assume they must be great for acquiring all that they have.

(1) Deuteronomy 8:11-20—Moses warned the people of Israel, saying, "Beware that thou forget not the Lord thy God, in not keeping his commandments, and his ordinances, and his statutes, which I command thee this day, lest, when thou hast eaten and art full and hast built goodly houses, and dwelt therein; and when thy herds and thy flocks multiply, and thy silver and thy gold are multiplied; and all that thou hast is multiplied; then thine heart be lifted up" (vv. 11-14). Moses told the people that they would receive wonderful things at the hand of God in the Promised Land. But he warned them that there would be a tendency to forget the source of their blessings. Instead they would think they had acquired those things based on their own abilities.

Then Moses said, "[You will] forget the Lord thy God, who brought thee forth out of the land of Egypt, from the house of bondage; who led thee through that great and terrible wilderness, wherein were fiery serpents, and scorpions, and drought, where there was no water; who brought thee forth water out of the rock of flint; who fed thee in the wilderness with manna, which thy fathers knew not, that he might humble thee, and that he might test thee, to do thee good at thy latter end" (vv. 14-16). Moses told them the day would come when they would forget what God had done for them and would believe they had done it themselves. They would forget that for forty years they had been absolutely dependent on God. Every good thing they ever had was from Him—every meal and every drop of water. But they would forget and become proud, as if they had survived all by themselves. Then Moses said, "Thou [will] say in thine heart, My power and the might of mine hand hath gotten me this wealth. But *thou shalt remember the Lord thy God; for it is he who giveth thee power to get wealth*, that he may establish his covenant which he swore unto thy fathers, as it is this day. And it shall be, if thou do at all forget the Lord thy God, and walk after other gods, and serve them, and worship them, I testify against you this day that ye shall surely perish. As the nations which the Lord destroyeth before your face, so shall ye perish, because ye would not be obedient unto the voice of the Lord your God" (vv. 17-20, emphasis added).

Everything we have God gave us. Are we parading our possessions as if we have obtained them ourselves with our own self-created abilities? If you lived in certain countries it wouldn't matter how creative you were, because the best you could do for yourself would be a two-room mud hut. Don't kid yourself about who the source is; it's not you.

(2) Isaiah 5:8—"Woe unto them who join house to house, who lay field to field, till there is no place, that they may be placed alone in the midst of the earth!" Woe to the person who buys more and more until he has crowded people so far out of

his life that he is totally alone with his possessions.

(3) Revelation 3:17—Christ rebuked the church at Laodicea, saying, "Thou sayest, I am rich, and increased with goods, and have need of nothing, and knowest not that thou art wretched, and miserable, and poor, and blind and naked."

The sin of economic pride is manifested first in boastfulness, then in the idea that you have acquired all you have on your own, and finally in the wastefulness of parading your riches rather than investing them in God's kingdom.

c) Pride in one's deeds

A braggart (Gk. *alazōn*) is one who makes more of himself than reality justifies, "ascribing to himself either more and better things than he has, or even what he does not possess at all" (Gerhard Delling, "*Alazōn*," *Theological Dictionary of the New Testament*, edited by Gerhard Kittel, vol. 1 [Grand Rapids: Eerdmans, 1965], pp. 226-27). Picture a stranger in town walking up to a man standing on the shore gazing at a fleet of ships in the harbor. He says, "Those are lovely ships; to whom do they belong?" The man answers, "Those are my ships. They have sailed the seven seas and carried the greatest of cargos." With that the man walks away. The stranger is so awestruck that he approaches a passerby and says to him, "Did you know that all those ships belong to that man over there?" The passerby looks toward the man and says, "Oh, no. He's the town fool. Those ships don't belong to him. He's nothing but a braggart."

We may catch ourselves saying things about ourselves that aren't true. It's amazing how the facts change the further we are from an actual event. The story gets better and better year after year. Every time you tell it there's a new wrinkle. Verbal pride consists of boasting and arrogance. The idea is to make sure you tell everyone what you want them to hear.

(1) Bragging about what we have done

> There is a tendency in human nature to tell people what we have done. I certainly fight that. People get into a conversation and soon they're trying to top each other about the things they've done. In 1 Samuel 2:3 Hannah says, "Talk no more so exceeding proudly, let not arrogancy come out of your mouth; for the Lord is a God of knowledge, and by him actions are weighed." God knows the truth about what you really did. Proverbs 27:2 says, "Let another man praise thee, and not thine own mouth."
>
> As a test, try to get through an entire week without once talking about what you've done. Try to last an afternoon for a starter. When people don't talk about what they've done, the very absence of bragging says volumes about their character.

(2) Bragging about what we're going to do

> People boast about many things they would like to do, such as telling off someone they don't like or building a big business and making millions of dollars. First Kings 20:11 says, "Let not him that girdeth on his armor boast himself as he that putteth it off." A soldier wasn't to boast before the battle; only after it was over might he have a reason to boast. Psalm 12:3 says, "The Lord shall cut off all flattering lips, and the tongue that speaketh proud things." What a vivid picture! There's no reason for us to brag about what we've done or what we will do.

d) Pride in one's class

(1) The world's perspective

When people reach a certain level in society, they have a tendency to look down on people at lower levels. They tend to think of them as lower-class, as people they don't want in their neighborhood. They tend to invite to dinner only those who are at a certain strata in society—certainly not someone who might dishonor their home. They certainly don't want to spend time with anyone who isn't a good conversationalist. But all those attitudes are sin—the sin of pride.

(2) God's perspective

Anyone who thinks like that has forgotten something important: God loves poor people. In fact, Jesus was one of them when He was in the world.

(*a*) James 2:2-4, 6-8—"If there come into your assembly a man with a gold ring, in fine apparel, and there come in also a poor man in vile raiment, and ye have respect to him that weareth the fine clothing, and say unto him, Sit thou here in a good place; and say to the poor, Stand thou there, or sit here under [by] my footstool, are ye not then partial in yourselves, and are become judges with evil thoughts? . . . Do not rich men oppress you, and draw you before the judgment seats? Do not they blaspheme that worthy name by which ye are called? If ye fulfill the royal law according to the scripture, Thou shalt love thy neighbor as thyself, ye do well." There is to be equality among all men and women.

(*b*) Psalm 10:2—"The wicked in his pride doth persecute the poor." You might say you would never persecute a poor man. But you do persecute him when you don't let him into your world, don't love him, and don't share your abundance to meet his need.

e) Pride in one's appearance

(1) The temptation

I believe people ought to dress appropriately—to have a sense of propriety. If people look too bad they may call attention to themselves in a negative way. That's what the Pharisees did. Whenever they wanted to appear pious, they put on old, torn clothes and put ashes on their head. They looked so terrible that the people would judge them to be holy since they appeared to have no concern for worldly things. But that wasn't holiness; Jesus said it was hypocrisy.

In our society advertisers tempt us to call attention to ourselves by what we wear. And they're very effective. We buy many of the useless things Madison Avenue promotes so we can show off.

(2) The confrontation

The apostle Paul had to address this particular problem. In his day, when the women wanted to show off their wealth they revealed it by the ornaments they put in their hair. A woman would let her hair grow long, then wind it up with all sorts of things, such as gold and tortoise-shell combs, stick pins, and pearls. She would have a literal fortune on her head. To counteract such ostentatious displays in the church, Paul said that women should "adorn themselves in modest apparel . . . not with braided hair, or gold, or pearls, or costly array, but with good works" (1 Tim. 2:9-10). Yet this admonition isn't limited to women; men also must be careful how they dress.

Lucifer was the most beautiful creature God ever made, but his beauty was his downfall (Ezek. 28:11-19). God has made some of you lovely to look at, and Satan can use that to make you prideful. Such pride causes people to become haughty, boastful, and indulgent, desiring to show themselves off as better than others. But it's an evil thing (Isa. 3:16-26).

f) Pride in one's position

(1) Described

Everyone holds a certain position in life, and everyone is tempted to take advantage of it. In any position of leadership, whether it's in your home, at your job, at school, or in a group of peers, you can always be tempted to oppress people with an exaggerated sense of your own importance.

(2) Displayed

(*a*) Revelation 18:7-8—The apostle John personified the pride of Babylon: "How much she hath glorified herself, and lived luxuriously, so much torment and sorrow give her; for she saith in her heart, I sit a queen, and am no widow, and shall see no sorrow. Therefore shall her plagues come in one day, death, and mourning, and famine, and she shall be utterly burned with fire; for strong is the Lord God who judgeth her."

(*b*) Acts 12:21-23—"Upon a set day Herod, arrayed in royal apparel, sat upon his throne, and made an oration unto them. And the people gave a shout, saying, It is the voice of a god, and not of a man. And immediately an angel of the Lord smote him, because he gave not God the glory; and he was eaten of worms, and died."

(*c*) Daniel 4:30-33, 37—"The king [Nebuchadnezzar] spoke, and said, Is not this great Babylon, that I have built for the house of the kingdom by the might of my power, and for the honor of my majesty?" (v. 30). Then God took the kingdom away from Nebuchadnezzar and turned him into a raving maniac. Nebuchadnezzar acted like an animal—his fingernails grew like the claws of a bird, his hair grew like that of an animal, and he was wet with the dew (vv. 31-33). Then in verse 37 a restored Nebuchadnezzar says, "[I] praise and extol and honor the King of heaven, all whose works are truth, and his ways justice; and those that walk in pride he is able to abase." Nebuchadnezzar got the message.

g) Pride in one's social status

In a sense this is like pride in one's class, only you demand to be treated a certain way. As you move up the social ladder, you expect a certain kind of treatment. If your waiter is one minute late, you indignantly wonder why he's treating you like an ordinary customer. As people move up they tend to expect the best of everything. But that's an erroneous view of one's worth. There's certainly nothing wrong with what God provides, but your perspective can be distorted.

(1) Luke 14:8-10—The religious leaders always wanted to hold the chief seats in the synagogue. They wanted to lord their authority over everyone and wanted people to recognize them. So Jesus told a story that illustrated the right attitude: "When thou art bidden by any man to a wedding, sit not down in the chief seat, lest a more honorable man than thou be bidden of him; and he that bade thee and him come and say to thee, Give this man place; and thou begin with shame to take the lowest place. But when thou art bidden, go and sit down in the lowest place that, when he that bade thee cometh, he may say unto thee, Friend, go up higher; then shalt thou have honor in the presence of them that dine with thee."

(2) Matthew 23:6-7—Of the scribes and Pharisees Jesus said, "[They] love the uppermost places at feasts, and the chief seats in the synagogues, and greetings in the market places, and to be called by men, Rabbi, Rabbi."

Social pride is an overwhelming desire to attain worldly honor and glamour. It's the temptation to become important in society.

h) Pride in one's external spirituality

Above all types of pride I think this is the worst. In Matthew 23:27 Jesus says, "Woe unto you, scribes and Pharisees, hypocrites! For ye are like whited sepulchers, which indeed appear beautiful outward, but are within full of dead men's bones, and of all uncleanness." Throughout the gospels He condemned the sin but loved the sinner. But with those hypocrites He condemned both sin and sinner alike because they pretended to be spiritual when they weren't.

We can look spiritual by carrying a notebook and a Bible, yet be a devil inside. There's nothing wrong with looking spiritual on the outside, as long as the attitude of your heart matches the image you're projecting.

i) Pride in one's intellect

After listening to the bad theology of his friends, Job said, "Ye are the people, and wisdom shall die with you" (Job. 12:2). It's so easy to be intellectually smug and think that you have your theology together and that you know everything.

Conclusion

Satan will tempt you to be proud about what you can do, how much you make, what you say, where you are in society, what you look like, what position you hold, what you desire socially, how you act spiritually, and what you know. Beware, for giving in to those temptations will tear humility from your grasp. And when you lose humility, you miss the first step in walking worthy of Christ.

Focusing on the Facts

1. According to 1 Peter 5:5, how should pastors and leaders handle the recognition they receive from their people (see p. 55)?
2. What is one of God's purposes for bringing problems into our lives (see p. 56)?
3. Explain how Satan tempts us to be proud of our strengths (see pp. 56-57).
4. Name two of Paul's strengths. According to 1 Corinthians 2:1-5, what was his attitude about them (see pp. 57-58)?
5. Any talent useful to God is a gift of _____ _____ _____ (see p. 58).
6. How is pride regarding one's economic status manifested (see p. 60)?
7. What are two ways that pride in one's accomplishments manifests itself? Explain (see p. 61).
8. Explain the temptation of pride in one's class (see p. 62).
9. What is God's perspective on different classes of people (see p. 62)?
10. In what way did Paul confront pride in one's appearance (1 Tim. 2:9-10; see p. 63)?
11. Give biblical examples of people who were proud of their position (see pp. 64-65).
12. How does pride in one's social status manifest itself (see p. 65)?
13. Describe pride in one's external spirituality (see p. 66).

Pondering the Principles

1. One of the greatest dangers Christians face in the United States is the temptation to be proud of their possessions and wealth. Even those who don't have much are conditioned by society to be proud of what they do have. How does that kind of pride manifest itself in your life? Read Deuteronomy 8:18 and Matthew 6:19-34. What kind of attitude does God want you to have? Make a daily practice of thanking God for all He has given you.

2. Take the test described on page 61. Beginning today, for the next week try not to talk about anything you have done or anything you plan to do that isn't strictly for informational purposes. For example, you may have to report to your boss about what you accomplished one day, but avoid all unnecessary

bragging. Assess what happens after a week. Then commit yourself to displaying that attitude every day.

3. Review the nine types of pride listed in this lesson. Which one are you tempted by the most? How does it manifest itself? Read Romans 12:3, 1 Corinthians 10:12, Galatians 6:3, and James 4:6. How might you apply those verses to your particular situation? Ask God for the help of His Spirit in overcoming pride in your life. Ask Him to continue to reveal the areas of your life that are affected by pride.

5
The Lowly Walk—Part 5

Outline

Introduction

Review
I. The Call to the Worthy Walk (v. 1)
II. The Characteristics of the Worthy Walk (vv. 2-3)
  A. Humility

Lesson
  B. Meekness
    1. The meaning of meekness
      a) The modern definition
      b) The Greek definition
        (1) In classical Greek
        (2) In the New Testament
          (*a*) Galatians 5:23
          (*b*) 1 Timothy 6:11-12
          (*c*) James 3:13, 17
        (3) In Aristotle's *Ethics*
          (*a*) Courage
          (*b*) Generosity
          (*c*) Meekness
    2. The models of meekness
      a) Jesus
        (1) When His Father was dishonored
          (*a*) By the moneychangers
          (*b*) By the Pharisees
        (2) When He Himself was dishonored

Introduction

Ephesians 4:1-3 reveals a basic truth about Christianity: the Christian life is not a matter of what you do but who you are. In verse 1 the apostle Paul begs believers to walk worthy of their calling in Christ. We have seen that that refers to our daily conduct and the attitude behind it. Performing the right deeds with the wrong attitude is hypocrisy.

It is possible to have what I call "action fruit"—such as praise (Heb. 13:15), giving (Phil. 4:17), evangelism (Rom. 1:13), and good works (Col. 1:10)—without "attitude fruit," which is the fruit of the Spirit: love, joy, peace, patience, gentleness, goodness, faith, meekness, and self-control (Gal. 5:22-23). If you have action fruit without attitude fruit, you become legalistic. But attitude fruit produces action fruit, and that's the right formula for true spirituality. The worthy walk begins with the right attitude. The Holy Spirit works through our attitudes to produce the appropriate actions. Ephesians 4:2-3 tells us that to walk worthy means we must begin with these attitudes: humility, meekness, patience, love, and maintaining unity.

Many Christians think the essence of the Christian life is going to church, putting money in the offering plate, owning and perhaps occasionally reading a Bible, not swearing or drinking, and not committing any crime. But such external behavior is only that—external behavior. It is not necessarily a manifestation of who we are in Christ. God is not concerned about what we do apart from who we are, because who we are determines what we do.

70

I. THE CALL TO THE WORTHY WALK (v. 1; see pp. 26-31)

II. THE CHARACTERISTICS OF THE WORTHY WALK (vv. 2-3)

A. Humility (see pp. 44-49; 56-66)

Lesson

B. Meekness

Meekness is a by-product of humility. If we're to walk worthy as exalted children of God, heirs of the kingdom, and inheritors of all spiritual blessings in the heavenlies, we must be meek.

1. The meaning of meekness

   a) The modern definition

   A common dictionary definition of meekness is "a deficiency of spirit." However, Galatians 5:23 refers to meekness as a fruit of the Spirit. When true meekness is produced by the Spirit of God, it is a valuable virtue. Although the world tends to misperceive it as cowardice, timidity, or a lack of strength, that's not how the Bible defines meekness.

   b) The Greek definition

   The Greek word translated "meekness" (*prautēs*) refers to something mild and gentle. It means "to be gentle-hearted." A meek person is the opposite of someone who is vindictive or who harbors bitterness and resentment toward others. Meekness is characteristic of one who is opposed to vengeance or violence. It is a quiet, willing submission to God and to others. A meek person has a mild, gentle, non-retaliating spirit.

71

(1) In classical Greek

In ancient Greek sources *prautēs* was used to refer to a medicine that calmed and soothed the spirit. It also described a gentle breeze and a colt that had been broken and tamed—whose power and energy could now be channeled for useful purposes. And it was used of people who were friendly, tenderhearted, and gentle as opposed to hard, rough, coarse, or violent.

(2) In the New Testament

Meekness is a godly characteristic. Zephaniah 2:3 tells us to seek meekness. *Prautēs* is used at least twelve times in the New Testament. It is extolled as a virtue in several key passages.

(a) Galatians 5:23—Meekness is one of the fruits of the Holy Spirit.

(b) 1 Timothy 6:11-12—Paul said to Timothy, "Thou, O man of God . . . follow after righteousness, godliness, faith, love, patience, meekness. Fight the good fight of faith." A meek person is anything but a coward—he will fight for the right cause. A meek person has a gentle, pleasant spirit except when he ought to be angry.

(c) James 3:13—"Who is a wise man and endued with knowledge among you? Let him show out of a good life his works with meekness of wisdom." A meek person is wise.

Power Under Control

Since anger is not absent in a meek person, we can say that meekness is power under control.

1. Illustrated by a lion

There is a big difference between the lion running free in the wilds of Africa and the lion responding to the lion tamer at the circus. The lion in the circus has all the ferocity, energy, power, and strength of the one in the wild, but he is under the control of the lion tamer. The same is true of meekness. No longer does the lion in us seek its own causes and ends; it is submissive to the control of the Master. We don't lose our power; we harness it.

2. Illustrated by a horse

We see the same concept in the aforementioned usage of *prautēs* in reference to a horse. As long as the colt runs wild and free, its power is out of control and it serves no useful purpose to man. But when its power is brought under control, it can be used for helpful purposes.

3. Illustrated by the wind

When the wind blows with hurricane force, it wreaks havoc. But when it is a quiet breeze, it catches the windmill, which pumps the water, which waters the crops, which feed the masses.

Only power under control is useful. Within the heart of every believer is a lion. That lion has every right to roar and pounce upon its victim but not at its own discretion. It takes its direction from the Master, the Lord Jesus Christ Himself. Don't think for a moment that meekness is characterized by indifference, cowardice, weakness, or fearfulness. Meekness is not impotent or cowardly. Jesus was meek (Matt. 11:29), but He certainly wasn't impotent or cowardly.

Do Believers Have the Right to Get Angry?

A believer has every right to get angry—but only under certain conditions. Ephesians 4:26 says, "Be ye angry, and sin not." It's all right to get angry as long as you don't sin. That means there's a certain kind of anger that isn't sin. Anger for the right reason is power under control; anger for the wrong reason is power out of control.

1. Power out of control

Proverbs 25:28 says, "He that hath no rule over his own spirit is like a city that is broken down, and without walls." A person who is totally out of control is vulnerable. He falls into every temptation, failure, and weakness. He has no self-control, no rule over his own spirit.

2. Power under control

Proverbs 16:32 says, "He who ruleth his spirit [is better] than he that taketh a city." One who rules his spirit has power and energy, but it's under control. That same power and energy out of control creates nothing but chaos and sinfulness. People who become angry at everything know nothing of meekness. Meek people control their energies and strengths.

(3) In Aristotle's *Ethics*

The ancient Greek philosopher Aristotle established some definitions helpful in understanding meekness. In his *Nichomachean Ethics* Aristotle described virtue as the golden mean between two extremes, which are an excess of the virtue and a deficiency of it.

(a) *Courage* is the virtue between cowardice (the deficiency of courage) and foolhardiness (the excess of courage). Someone who is too courageous will get himself killed—that's foolhardiness. A person who has no courage at all is a coward.

(b) *Generosity* is the virtue between stinginess and wastefulness.

(c) *Meekness* is the virtue between indifference and a short temper. Aristotle said that the

74

gentle or meek person "is praised for being angry under the right circumstances and with the right people, and also in the right manner, at the right time, and for the right length of time" (translated by Martin Ostwald [Indianapolis: Bobbs-Merrill, 1962], p. 100). Meekness is indeed power under control.

What Is Righteous Indignation?

Meekness has its tough side. It doesn't back away from sin or cease to condemn evil. It is anger under God's control. A meek person submits himself to God, so he becomes angry over things that offend God, not himself. For example, if someone offends him personally he doesn't seek revenge. In *The Pilgrim's Progress* John Bunyan said, "He that is down needs fear no fall" ([Grand Rapids: Zondervan, 1976], p. 219). The meek person has nowhere to fall because he seeks nothing for himself. But when God is maligned, the lion in him roars. That's holy, righteous indignation. Meekness is a quiet spirit that doesn't retaliate when wronged. But when God is dishonored, that same quiet spirit exercises its power. Holy indignation under God's control reacts when it ought to react, for the right reasons, and for the right length of time.

2. The models of meekness

    a) Jesus

In 2 Corinthians 10:1 Paul speaks of the meekness of Christ. In Matthew 11:29 Jesus says, "I am meek and lowly in heart." Zechariah prophesied that the Messiah would come to Jerusalem meek and lowly, "riding upon an ass, and upon a colt, the foal of an ass" (9:9). He didn't ride into Jerusalem on a great white steed; He rode on the most common of animals.

(1) When His Father was dishonored

    (*a*) By the moneychangers

Jesus walked into the Temple, whipped the moneychangers, overturned their tables and their money, and chased their animals out of the Temple (John 2:15). He said, "Make not my Father's house an house of merchandise" (v. 16).

(*b*) By the Pharisees

Jesus also confronted the vile hypocrisy of the scribes and Pharisees. He called them "whited sepulchers, which indeed appear beautiful outward, but are within full of dead men's bones" (Matt. 23:27).

Jesus never spoke a word of retaliation or condemnation against anyone for something they had done to Him, but He spoke up when God's honor was at stake.

(2) When He Himself was dishonored

First Peter 2:21-23 says, "Christ also suffered for us, leaving us an example . . . who, when he was reviled, reviled not again." He cleansed the Temple of the moneychangers because they were defiling the Father's house. But while the temple of His body was being defiled as He hung on the cross, He said to the people who mocked Him, "Father, forgive them; for they know not what they do" (Luke 23:34). That's meekness—total selflessness. Jesus never reacted to personal dishonor, only that which dishonored the Father.

When the Jewish leaders and Roman soldiers came to capture Jesus in the Garden of Gethsemane, Jesus could have called the angels of heaven to His aid if He so desired. He said, "Thinkest thou that I cannot now pray to my Father, and he shall presently give me more than twelve legions of angels?" (Matt. 26:53). Since at that time a Roman legion consisted of 3,000 to 6,000 soldiers, He could have had as many as 72,000 angels on hand. Yet one would have been enough, since only one angel killed 185,000 Assyrians (Isa.

37:36). But Jesus wouldn't use that power for His own defense.

Jesus' meekness led Him to make a whip and defend God against those who were desecrating His name. But it also kept Him from seeking vengeance for any dishonor against Himself. Certainly we are tempted to strike back when something happens to us. But you need to remind yourself not to get angry about what your neighbor does to you, because what happens to you shouldn't matter. Since you are God's servant, your meekness should lead you to retaliate only when God's honor is at stake.

b) David

(1) His meekness in dealing with Saul

A good portion of 1 Samuel is devoted to David's flight from Saul. David knew he was the anointed king, and Saul knew that the kingdom would be taken from him and given to David (1 Sam. 15:23-28). On one occasion David and his men were hiding in a cave when Saul came in to relieve himself (1 Sam. 24:3). David knew he had the right to reign, and that Saul was trying to destroy that opportunity by killing him. In most cases men under similar circumstances would have sought revenge against Saul, especially when faced with such a prime opportunity. Most would have assumed that God had led Saul into the cave, and that it was the right moment to kill him. That's what David's men thought (v. 4). But "David arose, and cut off the skirt of Saul's robe stealthily" (v. 4). That's how David proved to Saul that he had been in the cave and could have killed him if he'd wanted. David had the power and the right to kill Saul, but he submitted his power to God's authority. David was zealous to protect God's honor, not his own. In Psalm 69:9 he says, "Zeal of thine house hath eaten me up; and the reproaches of those who reproached thee are fallen upon me."

77

(2) His meekness in dealing with Shimei

David's evil, rebellious son Absalom tried to take
his father's kingdom away from him (2 Sam. 15:1-
12). As a result David had to flee for his life (vv.
13-23). He became a laughingstock to some of the
people because he ran from his own son. During
the time of David's retreat into the wilderness,
"there came out a man of the family of the house
of Saul, whose name was Shimei, the son of Gera;
he came forth, and cursed continuously as he
came. And he cast stones at David" (2 Sam. 16:5-
6). David's nephew Abishai then asked for per-
mission to cut off Shimei's head (v. 9). But David
told Abishai to leave him alone (v. 11). That's
power under control. (However it's sad to note
that David apparently lost some of that control at
the end of his life, judging by his attitude toward
Shimei in 1 Kings 2:8.)

David didn't seek vengeance for himself. If Shimei
had thrown rocks at Saul, he would have been killed
on the spot. The difference between David and Saul
is simple: they both had power, but one had it under
control while the other's was out of control. One was
like a fortified city; the other like a city with no walls
(Prov. 25:28). On one occasion Saul was so out of
control that he was prepared to kill his own son over
a minor issue (1 Sam. 14:36-45). Yet when David's
son rebelled against him, David said he would have
died for Absalom's sake (2 Sam. 18:33). Saul wouldn't
allow anyone to offend him, even his own son. David
could be offended by anyone, even his own son, and
was willing to lose his own life.

c) Moses

Numbers 12:3 says, "The man Moses was very meek,
above all the men who were upon the face of the
earth." Moses was the meekest man who ever lived.
And most of us wouldn't think of Moses as a Caspar
Milquetoast but as a fearless, bold, confrontive, courageous man of conviction. Indeed, he was a dynamic
and powerful leader.

(1) His anger

Throughout his life Moses exploded in anger—both righteous and unrighteous.

(a) Murder

The first incident occurred when he saw an Egyptian abusing a Jewish worker, so Moses killed the Egyptian (Ex. 2:11-12).

(b) Confrontation

After God had refined Moses' character for forty years in the wilderness, Moses returned to Egypt and told Pharaoh, the greatest monarch in the world at the time, to let his people go (Ex. 5:1). Moses wasn't afraid to face Pharaoh, nor was he afraid to make demands of him.

When Moses found the Israelites engaged in idolatry and debauchery, he smashed the law of God in his fury and rebuked the people (Ex. 32:19-20).

Moses was bold, combative, and confrontive. He had outbursts of righteous anger. He certainly wasn't a timid coward. For a third of his life he exercised authority over a couple of million people. Although he was bold and strong, the Bible tells us he was the meekest man who ever lived. Why? Because his anger was aroused when God was dishonored, not when he wanted to defend himself.

(2) His confidence

Moses' confidence wasn't in himself. When God appeared to Moses in the midst of a burning bush and called him to serve, Moses said, "Who am I, that I should go unto Pharaoh, and that I should bring forth the children of Israel out of Egypt?" (Ex. 3:11). But God assured him that He would lead them, and gave him a rod that represented His power (Ex. 4:2-9).

How Do You Know If You're Meek?

Here are some practical questions to ask yourself:

1. Do you experience self-control?

Is your anger always under control? Do you rule your own spirit (Prov. 16:32), or does your temper often flare up? When your spouse says something to you that could start an argument, do you immediately defend yourself or do you defer when possible?

2. Are you angry only when God is dishonored?

The things that should make you angry are the things that dishonor God, mar His reputation, and despise His name. Do you get angry about sin or when God's Word is perverted by false doctrines and false teachers? Do you get angry with people who claim to know Christ but obviously don't? We must gently exhort those who oppose us, but we have every right to be angry when God is dishonored.

3. Do you respond humbly to God's Word?

James 1:21 says we are to "receive with meekness the engrafted word." Do you submit meekly to the Word of God no matter what it says?

4. Do you always seek to make peace?

Meek people are peacemakers. Ephesians 4:3 says they endeavor "to keep the unity of the Spirit in the bond of peace." If someone falls into sin, do you condemn that person or gossip about him or her? Or do you practice Galatians 6:1? There Paul says, "If a man be overtaken in a fault, ye who are spiritual restore such an one in the spirit of meekness." Are you a peacemaker? Meek people don't start fights; they end them.

5. Do you accept criticism without retaliation?

Whether the criticism is right or wrong, we need to accept it without retaliating. Whenever people write to criticize me, the Holy Spirit often leads me to write them back and thank them for their criticism (cf. 2 Tim. 2:24-25).

6. Do you have the right attitude toward non-Christians?

Peter said to "be ready always to give an answer to every man that asketh you a reason of the hope that is in you, with meekness and fear" (1 Pet. 3:15). It's easy for Christians to become smug. We can be tempted to look down on non-Christians and become proud of our spirituality, forgetting that before God graciously saved us we were in the same position as they.

Conclusion

The One who made the world, who formed the galaxies in space, who calls every star by name, who preserves innumerable orbits, who weighs the mountains on a scale, who holds the waters in the hollow of His hand, and before whom the inhabitants of the world are as grasshoppers, is meek and lowly. Can you be anything less? First Peter 3:4 speaks of, "The hidden man of the heart in that which is not corruptible, even the ornament of a meek and quiet spirit, which is in the sight of God of great price." May you be so adorned.

Focusing on the Facts

1. In the Christian life, what must precede godly action? Explain (see p. 70).
2. How does the world tend to define meekness (see p. 71)?
3. Define the Greek word *prautēs* (see p. 71).
4. In what ways was *prautēs* used in classical Greek (see p. 72)?
5. Since anger is not absent in a meek person, what is a good way to define meekness (see p. 72)?

6. How might you illustrate that definition (see p. 73)?
7. Do Christians have a right to get angry? Explain (see pp. 73-74).
8. How did Aristotle define meekness (see pp. 74-75)?
9. What is righteous indignation (see p. 75)?
10. How did Jesus react when God was dishonored? Cite some examples (see pp. 75-76).
11. How did Jesus react whenever He was dishonored (see pp. 76-77)?
12. Explain how David's dealing with Saul in 1 Samuel 24:4 exemplifies meekness (see p. 77).
13. Explain the difference between Saul and David in terms of their anger (see p. 78).
14. According to Numbers 12:3, who was the meekest man who ever lived (see p. 78)?
15. In what ways did he reveal his anger (see p. 79)?
16. Why was he considered the meekest man who ever lived (see p. 79)?
17. Cite the six questions you need to ask yourself to find out if you are meek (see pp. 80-81).

Pondering the Principles

1. Meekness is just one of the spiritual attitudes associated with the fruit of the Spirit in Galatians 5:22-23. Write down each attitude. With the help of a dictionary of New Testament words, write the definition of each. Next to each definition record how you see those attitudes manifested in your life. Then ask yourself, *Which of these attitudes do I struggle with most?* With the help of a concordance, look up the other uses of that word in the New Testament, so that you gain a comprehensive understanding of it. Ask God for His guidance in determining how to develop that attitude in yourself and become stronger in all the fruits of the Spirit.

2. Review the section on how to know if you are meek (see pp. 80-81). Ask yourself each of those questions, and record your honest appraisal. Which one of the questions did you have to answer with the strongest no? Since developing meekness will take time, concentrate on just that one aspect right now. Begin to think of ways you might develop a meek attitude in that particular area. For example, if you have difficulty accepting criti-

cism, you might look up all the times that Jesus was unjustly criticized to see how He responded. Then you could try to respond like He did whenever you are criticized. Again ask God for His guidance as you work on developing this important characteristic.

6
The Lowly Walk—Part 6

Outline

Review
I. The Call to the Worthy Walk (v. 1)
II. The Characteristics of the Worthy Walk (vv. 2-3)
   A. Humility
   B. Meekness

Lesson
   C. Patience
      1. The elements of patience
         a) Enduring negative circumstances
            (1) Abraham
            (2) Noah
            (3) Moses
            (4) The prophets
               (*a*) Jeremiah
               (*b*) Isaiah
            (5) Paul
               (*a*) Acts 20:23-24
               (*b*) Acts 21:11, 13
         b) Coping with difficult people
         c) Accepting God's plan for everything
      2. The example of patience
         a) Jesus endured negative circumstances
         b) Jesus coped with difficult people
         c) Jesus accepted God's plan for everything

D. Love
  1. The definition
  2. The distinctions
     a) *Eros*
     b) *Phileō*
     c) *Agapē*
  3. The description
E. Unity
  1. The need for diligence
  2. The work of the Spirit
  3. The bond of peace
III. The Cause of the Worthy Walk (vv. 4-6)
  A. The Holy Spirit (v. 4)
     1. One body
     2. One Spirit
     3. One hope
  B. The Lord Jesus Christ (v. 5)
     1. One Lord
        a) Acts 4:12
        b) Galatians 1:9
        c) Mark 13:21-22
        d) Romans 10:12
        e) Colossians 2:9-10
     2. One faith
     3. One baptism
  C. The Father (v. 6)

Conclusion

Review

We have seen that the Christian life is first an issue of who we are. What we do follows (see pp. 36-42). We can't begin to see the power of God in our lives until we're strengthened by God's Spirit in the inner man (Eph. 3:16). The worthy walk begins in the inner man, and that's the subject of Ephesians 4:1-6.

I. THE CALL TO THE WORTHY WALK (v. 1; see pp. 26-31)

"I therefore, the prisoner of the Lord, beseech you that ye walk worthy of the vocation to which ye are called."

II. THE CHARACTERISTICS OF THE WORTHY WALK (vv. 2-3)

"With all lowliness and meekness, with long-suffering, forbearing one another in love, endeavoring to keep the unity of the Spirit in the bond of peace."

The goal of the worthy walk is unity. God's primary direction for the church is that we be one. Only then will the world recognize the supernatural origin of the church (see p. 43), and only then will the church rightly manifest Christ to the world (see p. 44). When the apostle Paul looked at the church he said, "There is neither Jew nor Greek, there is neither bond nor free, there is neither male nor female; for ye are all one in Christ Jesus" (Gal. 3:28). But how do we establish that unity?

A. Humility (see pp. 44-49; 56-66)

B. Meekness (see pp. 71-81)

Lesson

C. Patience

The Greek word translated "long-suffering" (*makrothumia*) means "patient" or "long-tempered." A patient person doesn't have a short fuse or lose his temper.

1. The elements of patience

    a) Enduring negative circumstances

    (1) Abraham

    Abraham received a promise from God: "In blessing I will bless thee, and in multiplying I will multiply thy seed as the stars of the heaven, and as the sand which is upon the seashore" (Gen. 22:17). Hebrews 6:15 says of Abraham, "After he had patiently endured [*makrothumia*], he obtained the promise." God had promised Abraham many descendants, yet he and Sarah had no children;

she was barren, and Abraham himself was over ninety years old (Rom. 4:19). Nevertheless "he staggered not at the promise of God through unbelief, but was strong in faith, giving glory to God" (v. 20). He believed God in the midst of negative circumstances, and ultimately God fulfilled His promise.

(2) Noah

In Noah's day rain had never fallen upon the earth. Yet when God instructed him to build a boat in the desert, Noah patiently endured for 120 years and built the ark (Gen. 6:3, 13-14; cf. 1 Pet. 3:20).

(3) Moses

Moses chose "to suffer affliction with the people of God than to enjoy the pleasures of sin for a season" (Heb. 11:25). He endured. A patient person has the ability to endure any circumstance without giving up or losing control.

(4) The prophets

James 5:10 speaks of "the prophets who have spoken in the name of the Lord, for an example of suffering affliction, and of patience [makrothumia]."

(a) Jeremiah

God informed Jeremiah that he would spend his life preaching, although the people wouldn't listen to him nor would the nation turn from its evil practices (Jer. 1:5-19). But Jeremiah was faithful and endured hatred, persecution, rejection, and unbelief. He was a truly humble man. He endured any circumstance to further the cause of God.

(*b*) Isaiah

> God gave similar instructions to Isaiah. He told him that in spite of the message he preached, the nation would continue to fall deeper into sin (Isa. 6:9-12). But Isaiah endured all the negative circumstances.

(5) Paul

> (*a*) Acts 20:23-24—Before going to Jerusalem, Paul said to the Ephesian elders, "The Holy Spirit witnesseth in every city, saying that bonds and afflictions await me. But none of these things move me, neither count I my life dear unto myself, so that I might finish my course with joy, and the ministry, which I have received of the Lord Jesus." Paul would endure anything to accomplish God's purposes.

> (*b*) Acts 21:11, 13—Agabus the prophet "took Paul's belt, and bound his own hands and feet, and said, Thus saith the Holy Spirit, So shall the Jews at Jerusalem bind the man that owneth this belt, and shall deliver him into the hands of the Gentiles" (v. 11). But Paul replied to those who therefore wanted to prevent him from going to Jerusalem, "What mean ye to weep and to break mine heart? For I am ready, not to be bound only but also to die at Jerusalem for the name of the Lord Jesus" (v. 13). All that mattered to Paul were the purposes, will, and work of God.

b) Coping with difficult people

Sometimes the problems in life are not our circumstances but the people around us. *Makrothumia* is used in Scripture to speak of patience with people as well as patience in circumstances. For example

1 Thessalonians 5:14 says, "Be patient toward all men." That is meekness applied—the spirit that refuses to retaliate. A patient person bears insult, injury, persecution, unfair treatment, slander, criticism, hatred, jealousy, and envy. Whatever people throw at us we should accept without bitterness or complaint.

When you come into contact with a truly patient person, you can't start a fight with him no matter how hard you try. You are forced to live in peace with him. Our normal reaction is to be defensive when we're provoked, which communicates that who we are and what we do is most important to us. But the important thing is to defend God, not ourselves.

People who criticize what I do help me whether they do it out of love or not. Criticism of my actions makes me rethink what I've done. That I can handle. But when someone impugns my motives, it's harder for me to take. Since it's almost impossible to state with certainty the motives of another, doing so is usually slander. But we really shouldn't be defensive about any kind of criticism. The patient person defends God, not himself, knowing that He will repay all wrongs at the right time.

c) Accepting God's plan for everything

A person who is long-suffering never argues with God's plan. He doesn't question circumstances, people, or God. A person who is long-suffering says, "Lord, if this is what You have planned for me, I'll obey You."

2. The example of patience

a) Jesus endured negative circumstances

Jesus came into the world having experienced only the glory of heaven. In His preincarnate state He knew face-to-face fellowship with God the Father (John 1:1-2). But He chose to leave a perfect environment where His name was always praised. He came into our world where men rejected Him, cursed Him, and ultimately crucified Him. Yet Jesus endured it all for our sake.

b) Jesus coped with difficult people

While Jesus hung on the cross bearing the sin of mankind, men were spitting at Him and mocking Him. Yet He said, "Father, forgive them; for they know not what they do" (Luke 23:34). The people God forgives end up in heaven. Jesus was asking God to bring His murderers to heaven to be with Him forever.

c) Jesus accepted God's plan for everything

In the Garden of Gethsemane Jesus said, "O my Father, if it be possible, let this cup pass from me; nevertheless, not as I will, but as thou wilt" (Matt. 26:39). He was able to endure unimaginable suffering because He knew it was God's will.

Jesus was characterized by humility, which produced meekness and patience.

The Key to Evangelism

The virtues of Ephesians 4:2-3 enable the church of Jesus Christ to offer a powerful testimony. Many of us think the key to evangelism is following a specific course or method, but the greatest message we have in this world is love and unity. The world wouldn't know how to handle us if we exemplified those qualities because it would be obvious that they came from a supernatural source. Though evangelistic methods are important, often they aren't as effective as they could be because of the church's poor reputation among unbelievers. It has been said that the church is like Noah's ark: if it weren't for the storm outside you couldn't stand the stink inside. That's an awful thing to say about the church. But if the church were full of people who manifested genuine humility, meekness, and long-suffering, the world would have a much greater respect for it.

Sir Henry Stanley traveled to Africa in 1872 to find Dr. David Livingstone, the famous missionary and explorer. After finding him,

91

Stanley spent several months with Livingstone, who by that time was an old man. Apparently Livingstone didn't say much to Stanley about spiritual things—he just continued about his business with the Africans. Stanley observed that throughout the months he watched him, Livingstone's habits were beyond his comprehension, especially his patience. Stanley could not understand his sympathy for the Africans, who had wronged Livingstone many times. For the sake of Christ and His gospel David Livingstone was patient, untiring, and eager. He spent himself for His Master. In his exciting account *How I Found Livingstone* Stanley wrote, "His religion is not of the theoretical kind, but is a constant, earnest, sincere practice. It is neither demonstrative nor loud, but manifests itself in a quiet practical way, and is always at work. . . . In him religion exhibits its loveliest features; it governs his conduct not only towards his servants but towards the natives . . . and all who come in contact with him" ([N.Y.: C. Scribner, 1913], pp. 428-34).

I'm not advocating that you never talk about the gospel. However, know that what you say will have a far greater impact when you live your life in harmony with what the gospel teaches. If the world could see a clear picture of Jesus Christ through the unity of the church and its humble, meek, patient people, our evangelism would be sped along on wings!

D. Love

"Forbearing one another in love" (v. 2) is a product of patience.

1. The definition

The Greek word translated "forbearing" means "suppressing with silence." It carries the idea of throwing a blanket over sin. First Peter 4:8 says, "Love shall cover the multitude of sins." Proverbs 10:12 says, "Hatred stirreth up strifes, but love covereth all sins." A person who has forbearing love not only endures whatever people do to him, but also loves them in spite of those things. You may be able to endure slander and persecution by your enemies, but are you able to love them?

2. The distinctions

There are three common Greek words for love: *eros, phileō,* and *agapē*.

a) *Eros*—This is the love that takes. A person who exhibits *eros* loves someone for what he can get out of that other person. It's love that's typical of the world—sexual and lustful. It's the kind of love that drives us toward self-gratification.

b) *Phileō*—This is the love of give and take. In other words, I love you because of what I get from you and what I can give to you. It's the give and take of friendship.

c) *Agapē*—This is the love that gives; there's no taking involved. It's the kind of love that seeks the highest good for another no matter what the cost. It is completely unselfish. God so loved mankind in this way that He "gave his only begotten Son" (John 3:16). Jesus said, "Greater love hath no man than this, that a man lay down his life for his friends" (John 15:13).

Agapē is the Greek word translated "love" in "forbearing love" (Eph. 4:2). It is unconquerable benevolence and invincible goodness.

3. The description

Perhaps the greatest description of forbearing love is in Matthew 5:43-48. Jesus said, "Ye have heard it hath been said, Thou shalt love thy neighbor, and hate thine enemy; but I say unto you, Love your enemies, bless them that curse you, do good to them that hate you, and pray for them who despitefully use you, and persecute you, that ye may be the sons of your Father, who is in heaven. . . . For if ye love them who love you, what reward have ye? Do not even the tax collectors the same? And if ye greet your brethren only, what do ye more than others? Do not even the heathen so? But be ye, therefore, perfect, even as your Father, who is in heaven, is perfect." How is God's perfection manifest? He loves the unlovable, including His enemies, in spite of what they do to Him.

Forbearing love was exemplified by Jesus as He hung on the cross and forgave His persecutors. It was similarly exemplified by Stephen, who, as he lay dying beneath the rocks with which he was stoned, looked up to heaven and said, "Lord, lay not this sin to their charge" (Acts 7:60).

Ephesians 4 tells us that the key to living the Christian life begins inside us with a commitment to be humble, meek, patient, and loving—all aspects of the fruit of the Spirit. Only the Holy Spirit can produce those things in you as you yield to Him.

E. Unity

Ephesians 4:3 says to endeavor "to keep the unity of the Spirit in the bond of peace." That's the goal—that's how God wants us to manifest Christ to the world. He doesn't want the church to be seen as one more social club. Rather it is to be seen as a divine institution of God, supernaturally born, supernaturally sustained, and having a supernatural destiny. Only when we are humble, meek, patient, and loving can we work at being unified.

1. The need for diligence

The Greek word translated "endeavoring" (*spoudazō*) means "to make haste," "to be zealous," "to be eager," or "to give diligence." In 2 Timothy 4:9 and Titus 3:12 Paul asks his servants to give diligence in coming to see him. In 2 Timothy 2:15 he says, "Study [be diligent] to show thyself approved unto God, a workman that needeth not to be ashamed."

Spoudazō calls for a strong commitment. Unity begins in the heart. The church will acquire unity when individual Christians commit themselves to walking worthy of Christ. We have to work at it. *The Theological Dictionary of the New Testament*, edited by Gerhard Kittel, describes

94

the noun form of *spoudazō* as "a 'holy zeal' which demands full dedication" (Günther Harder, "*Spoudazō, Spoudē*," vol. 7 [Grand Rapids: Eerdmans, 1971], p. 566).

Do Denominational Distinctives Divide?

I am grieved by all the disunity and discord in the church today. One of the main causes is the focus on denominational distinctives. The church should focus on biblical distinctives—on what will unite us, not divide us. We need to humble ourselves and learn to love each other. That won't happen by starting a global ecumenical movement, but it will happen when we become what God wants us to be. Working at unity is a full-time task that demands maximum dedication and obedience from every Christian.

2. The work of the Spirit

Often we focus on creating unity, but the Holy Spirit already has made us one in Christ. Ephesians 4:3 clarifies what our responsibility is to be: "Endeavoring to keep the unity of the Spirit." We either keep unity or destroy it.

First Corinthians 12:13 says, "By one Spirit were we all baptized into one body." Romans 8:9 says we are all indwelt by the same Spirit. Our unity is not organizational and ecumenical; it is personal and spiritual. We must seek to maintain it.

3. The bond of peace

The bond of peace is what holds unity together. The Greek word translated "bond" refers to a belt. It depicts the Body of Christ being wrapped with the belt of peace, a peace that is born of love. That's what Paul meant in Philippians 2:1-4 when he commanded us to have the same love for one another. We can have that kind of love if we're like Christ (v. 5). That means we must humble ourselves and focus on the needs of others.

True unity is based on true love, which is based on true patience, which is based on true meekness, which is born out of true humility.

III. THE CAUSE OF THE WORTHY WALK (vv. 4-6)

"There is one body, and one Spirit, even as ye are called in one hope of your calling; one Lord, one faith, one baptism, one God and Father of all, who is above all, and through all, and in you all."

Everything God ever designed for the church is based on the unity of the people. Paul listed seven *one's*, and each member of the Trinity is specifically involved in all seven.

A. The Holy Spirit (v. 4)

1. One body

There is one Body of Christ. There isn't a Presbyterian Body, a Baptist Body, a Methodist Body, and an Episcopalian Body; or one in California, one in Utah, and one in Kansas—there's just one Body. Galatians 3:28 says, "There is neither Jew nor Greek, there is neither bond nor free, there is neither male nor female; for ye are all one in Christ Jesus." There is only one Body, one church, and one head of that church. The entire book of Ephesians is based on that concept. Whatever your race, creed, culture, nationality, or language may be, when you become a Christian you become one with every other believer. Ephesians 3:15 says there is only one family of believers.

2. One Spirit

There is just one Holy Spirit, and all believers are indwelt by Him. First Corinthians 6:19 says, "Know ye not that your body is the temple of the Holy Spirit?" Ephesians 2:22 says that the church is "built together for an habitation of God through the Spirit." Individually we are the temple of the Spirit; collectively we are the habitation of the Spirit.

3. One hope

Ephesians 4:4 says, "Ye are called in one hope of your calling." We have only one eternal calling, only one eternal destiny. The Holy Spirit guarantees our heavenly hope. Ephesians 1:13-14 says we were "sealed with that Holy Spirit of promise, who is the earnest of our inheritance." The Greek word translated "earnest" (Gk., *arrabōn*) can refer to an engagement ring. The proof that God will bring us to the marriage supper of the Lamb is the Holy Spirit—He's our down payment, our first installment. He guarantees our eternal inheritance.

Ephesians 4:4 delineates the Holy Spirit's ministry to us. We are placed into "one body" by the Holy Spirit, "one Spirit" indwells us, and our "one hope" is guaranteed by the Holy Spirit.

B. The Lord Jesus Christ (v. 5)

Verse 5 speaks of "one Lord, one faith, one baptism."

1. One Lord

We have one Lord.

   a) Acts 4:12—"Neither is there salvation in any other; for there is no other name under heaven given among men, whereby we must be saved."

   b) Galatians 1:9—"If any man preach any other gospel unto you . . . let him be accursed."

   c) Mark 13:21-22—Christ warned, "If any man shall say to you, Lo, here is Christ; or, lo, he is there; believe him not. For false Christs and false prophets shall rise, and shall show signs and wonders, to seduce, if it were possible, even the elect."

   d) Romans 10:12—"There is no difference between the Jew and the Greek; for the same Lord over all is rich unto all that call upon him."

e) Colossians 2:9-10—"In him dwelleth all the fullness of the Godhead bodily. And ye are complete in him."

2. One faith

The faith to which Paul refers is the content of Scripture. There may be many denominations and churches, but there is only one true Christian faith. Jude said, "Ye should earnestly contend for the faith which was once delivered unto the saints" (v. 3).

3. One baptism

This refers to water baptism. Some claim it refers to Spirit baptism, but that was referred to in verse 4 as "one body." We all were placed into the Body of Christ by the baptism of the Spirit (1 Cor. 12:13).

When a person comes to believe in the only true Lord, he should be baptized as a public expression of his faith. Public baptism was an essential part of the early church's testimony to the world. It is no less essential today. This one baptism is done "in the name of the Lord" (Acts 10:48), specifically "in the name of the Father, and of the Son, and of the Holy Spirit" (Matt. 28:19).

C. The Father (v. 6)

"One God and Father of all, who is above all, and through all, and in you all."

There is only one God—there are no others. Throughout the Old Testament God explicitly states that He is the only God. Deuteronomy 6:4 says, "The Lord our God is one Lord." As Christians we have the same Father. He is "above all," which means He is the sovereign Creator and controller of the universe. He is "through all," which means He is the providential upholder of the universe. And He is "in you all," which refers to His personal, indwelling presence.

Conclusion

Ephesians 4 describes the essentials of the Christian faith as "one." That's because God wants us to be one. To do that we have to look inside ourselves. We must begin with humility, which comes from a proper self-awareness, Christ-awareness, and God-awareness. Humility produces meekness, which produces patience, which produces love. Only when we possess those virtues can we maintain the unity of the Spirit in the bond of peace. As a result the world will see that we are different—that we are supernatural. Perhaps, like Sir Henry Stanley, they will be attracted to Christ because of our worthy walk. May it be so.

Focusing on the Facts

1. Define "long-suffering" (see p. 87).
2. What are three elements of patience (see pp. 87-90)?
3. Explain how Abraham stands out as an illustration of patience (see pp. 87-88).
4. Give other biblical examples of those who exhibited similar patience (see pp. 88-89).
5. How does someone who is patient relate to people (see pp. 89-90)?
6. How does a person who is patient react to God's will (see p. 90)?
7. How did Jesus fulfill the three elements of patience (see pp. 90-91)?
8. What is more important than methods and training in evangelism? Explain (see pp. 91-92).
9. What does "forbearing love" mean (see p. 92)?
10. What are the three common Greek words which are translated "love"? Define each one (see p. 93).
11. Which Greek word for love does Paul use in Ephesians 4:2 (see p. 93)?
12. How is God's perfection manifested (Matt. 5:43-48; see pp. 93-94)?
13. What is God's goal for the church (Eph. 4:3; see p. 94)?
14. What does the Greek word translated "endeavoring" call for (see p. 94)?

15. How is unity in the church created? What is our responsibility with regard to unity (see p. 95)?
16. What holds our unity together? Explain (see p. 95).
17. According to Ephesians 4:4, what is the Holy Spirit's ministry to us (see p. 96)?
18. What is the "faith" referred to in Ephesians 4:5 (see p. 98)?
19. What kind of "baptism" does Ephesians 4:5 refer to? Explain (see p. 98).
20. Explain the meaning of the phrases "above all," "through all," and "in you all" in Ephesians 4:6 (see p. 98).

Pondering the Principles

1. Review the elements of patience (see pp. 87-90). How do you usually respond to negative circumstances? How do you respond to criticism, especially criticism of your motives? How do you view God's immediate plan for your life? What can you apply to your life from Christ's example (see pp. 90-91)? Often we struggle with understanding why God allows difficult circumstances or people into our lives, so we question His plan. But who are we to question God? Read Isaiah 40:6-31. Get your focus off yourself and onto God, who allows us to mount up with wings like eagles so we won't grow weary.

2. According to Matthew 5:43-48, a true test of your Christianity is your willingness to love your enemies. What are some reasons that God wants us to love our enemies as well as our neighbors? Do you have a genuine love for your enemies? Think of specific people with whom you have difficulty getting along. What are some good ways you might begin to show love toward them? Make the commitment to follow through on those ideas.

Scripture Index

Topical Index

Generosity, definition of, 74
God
    awareness of, 27-28, 33, 49
    oneness of, 98
    triune nature of. *See* Trinity
    unity and. *See* Unity
God-consciousness. *See* God
Government, conformity to, 8
Grace, law vs., 28

Harder, Günther, on *spoudazō*
    (holy zeal), 94-95
Holy Spirit, the
    oneness of, 96-97
    unity and. *See* Unity
Humility
    blessing of, 41-42
    definition of, 44-45, 48
    developing, 55-56, 68
    exaltation and, 24
    Jesus', 37, 45, 46
    John the Baptist's, 46
    John's, 47
    manifestations of, 48-49
    Mark's, 47
    Mary's (Martha's sister), 47
    Matthew's, 47
    menaces to, 56-66
    Paul's, 27-28, 46, 50
    proverbs on, 41
    salvation and, 42
    standard of, 37
    virtue of, 41
    See also Meekness, Pride

Identity, need for. *See*
    Conformity
Indignation. *See* Anger
Initiations. *See* Fraternities
Intellect. *See* Knowledge
Isaiah, patience of. *See* Patience

Jeremiah, patience of. *See*
    Patience

Jesus Christ
    example of. *See* Humility,
        Meekness, Patience
    humility of. *See* Humility
    meekness of. *See* Meekness
    oneness of, 97-98
    patience of. *See* Patience
    position in. *See* Position vs.
        practice in Christ
    unity and. *See* Unity
John, humility of. *See* Humility
John the Baptist, humility of.
    See Humility

Kittel, Gerhard
    on *alazōn* (braggart), 60
    on *spoudazō* (holy zeal), 94-95
Knowledge
    accountability to, 25-26
    peril of, 25-26
    pride in, 66
    priority of, 15-19
    protection of, 24-25, 32
    See also Wisdom

Law of God, grace vs., 28
Leadership, humility of church,
    55
Livingstone, David, his impact
    on Stanley, 91-92, 99
Love
    definition of, 92
    description of, 93-94
    types of, 93

MacArthur, John
    battling pride in preaching,
        56-57
    fraternity and club member-
        ship of, 9
    impassioned preaching of, 23
    most humiliating experience
        of, 49

108

Scripture
  accountability to, 25-26
  applying, 20, 32
  knowing, 15-19, 24-26, 32
  reading, 18, 20
  studying, 18, 20
Self-awareness, 48-50
Self-control. *See* Meekness
Sin, protection against, 24-25, 32
Snobbery. *See* Social class, Social status
Social class, pride in one's, 62
Social status, pride in one's, 65-66
Sororities. *See* Fraternities
Spirituality, pride in one's external, 66
Sports, conformity in, 8
Stanley, Henry, his admiration of Livingstone, 91-92, 99
Status. *See* Social status

Talents. *See* Abilities
Teaching, responsibility of, 16
Trinity, work of the in bringing about unity, 96-98

Unity
  importance of, 43-44, 94-95, 99
  personal responsibility for, 51
  the Trinity's production of, 95-98

Walk, the Christian
  call to, 26-31
  cause of, 96-99
  characteristics of. *See* Humility, Meekness, Patience, Love, Unity
  definition of, 36
  essence of, 70
  power of, 27
  results of, 19
  the Trinity and, 96-99
Wisdom
  protection of, 24-25
  searching for, 15-16
  value of, 24-25
  See also Knowledge
Word of God. *See* Scripture
Work
  conformity at, 8
  pride at, 64-65
Worthy walk. *See* Walk, the Christian